before the Featherweight

Sewhandy

Volume 2
Maintenance & Repair

Darrel P. Kaiser

Published September 2007
Darrel P. Kaiser

Darrel Kaiser Books
www.DarrelKaiserBooks.com
email:Dar-Bet@att.net

First Printing

ISBN 978-0-6151-6967-5

Notice

before the Featherweight – Sewhandy Volume 2 explains the basic maintenance and repair that might be needed while owning a *Sewhandy* sewing machine. Both mechanical and electrical theory and operation with schematics and diagrams are presented.

This book also explains the basic and logical process of troubleshooting and fault diagnosis. Specific sewing faults are also discussed with the applicable *Sewhandy* mechanical functions and areas identified.

This information is not an "authority" for you to perform any maintenance or repairs. It is not a "recommendation" for you to perform any maintenance or repairs. All or some of the procedures explained in this book may be beyond your training and/or capabilities. If so, I strongly recommend that you have a professional sewing machine technician service your *Sewhandy*. The intent of this book is for educational purposes only.

Always remember to use safety equipment and follow all safety instructions if performing any maintenance or repair. A chapter on electrical and mechanical safety is provided to educate you, though it is not all-inclusive. It is your responsibility to utilize proper safety equipment and the safest procedure if you choose to perform any maintenance actions.

No warranty or representation, express or implied, with respect to accuracy, completeness, or usefulness of the information contained in this document, or use of any information, apparatus, method, or process disclosed in this document that may infringe on privately owned rights.

No liability is assumed with respect to the use of, or for damages resulting from the use of, any information, apparatus, method or process disclosed in this book.

See www.SewhandySewingMachine.com or feel free to email me at Dar-Bet@att.net for any additional information or assistance with your *Sewhandy*.

I also provide maintenance, repair, and restoration in my workshop thru my website:

www.SewingMachineTech.com

I welcome any and all discussion as to the "facts" or validity of my conclusions. Specific reference information is available on request; email me at Dar-Bet@att.net .

The Author

Darrel P. Kaiser has been professionally troubleshooting electrical, electronic, and mechanical components and systems for the US Government for the last 37 years. During those years, he also trained with PFAFF in Germany and Bernina USA in the art of professional sewing machine repair, and continues repair and restoration even today.

He has also been researching the development of the Germanic peoples and his ancestors for over 10 years. While living for over two years in Germany, Darrel "walked the lanes" and did on-site research in the villages of his ancestors.

After all those years of troubleshooting and repair, he turned to teaching at a Government University and writing technical books. Out of his research came his first book on Germanic History and Genealogy, *"Origins and Ancestors Families Karle & Kaiser of the German-Russian Volga Colonies."*

Darrel has also written and published numerous other books on German and Russian History, Politics, Religion, and Ancestry; a book on the Watercolor quilts of Betty Kaiser, a book on basic electrical troubleshooting, a book on sewing machine troubleshooting, two books on the SINGER 221 *Featherweight*, and two books on the STANDARD *Sewhandy* and GE *MODEL A* sewing machines. This book's final pages show all the titles.

For more on his research into German and Russian History and Genealogy, visit:

www.Volga-Germans.com

For more on his books on Troubleshooting, visit:

www.BasicTroubleshooting.com

For more on his books about Sewing Machines, visit:

www.SewingMachineTech.com

For more on his books about the STANDARD *Sewhandy* and GE *MODEL A* sewing machines, visit:

www.SewhandySewingMachines.com

For more information on all of his books, visit:

www.DarrelKaiserBooks.com

Preface

Originally, this book "before the Featherweight – *Sewhandy*" was written as one volume. After months of research and writing, I realized that documenting the *Sewhandy* sewing machine properly was going to cover over 500 pages. For that reason, "before the Featherweight – *Sewhandy*" has been published in two volumes.

Volume 1 covers the history of the life of the *Sewhandy*, i.e. prior to the design (early 1920's) thru the end of production (mid 1938). Also covered are associated patents, identification of your model, a sew-off comparison of an OSANN SINGER *Sewhandy* with a SINGER 221 Featherweight, and parts availability listing.

The original reason for Volume 1 was the recurring gossip and speculation that the Standard "*Sewhandy*" machine was possibly the forerunner of the SINGER Featherweight. Volume 1 was to either verify or dispel those rumors with an explanation using all information presently available.

While writing the original manuscript, I came to the conclusion that the *Sewhandy* sewing machine is a remarkable product. The original maintenance manual was not very informative, and some conclusions have surfaced about the *Sewhandy* that are not based on fact, but on a lack of correct information, i.e. required maintenance and lubrication requirements.

Volume 2 covers maintenance and repair of all *Sewhandy* models, mechanical theory of operation, electrical theory of operation, plus advice on buying, restoration, shipping, and replaceable consumables. Also included is identification of your model, a specification comparison of an **OSANN SINGER** *Sewhandy* with a **SINGER 221** Featherweight, and parts availability listing.

The reason for Volume 2 was to provide maintenance and repair information for all the *Sewhandy* models using modern lubricants and components.

Most of the information provided in both Volumes has been verified as fact thru multiple sources. I have attempted to be as accurate as possible; however, my accuracy is directly dependent on the accuracy of all the sources that have provided information over the past 80 years.

A small percentage of the information provided in both Volumes is based on a single source, or my assumptions from a number of sources. Again, I have attempted to be as accurate as possible in my assumptions and conclusions, however my accuracy is directly dependent on information that is 70 to 80 years old.

Note that when I use the term "*Sewhandy*" in both volumes, I am referring to all models of the

Sewhandy to include the GENERAL ELECTRIC *MODEL A*.

If I am referring to a specific model *Sewhandy*, I will add the manufacturer, i.e. STANDARD, FREDERICK OSANN, GE (GENERAL ELECTRIC), or OSANN SINGER.

I welcome any and all discussion as to the "facts" or validity of my conclusions. Specific reference information is available on request; email me at **Dar-Bet@att.net** .

Frederick and Edward Sr, ca 1933

My sincere thanks to Robert Osann Jr. and Edward R. Osann for their assistance with the research into the history and development of the *Sewhandy* and the FREDERICK OSANN Company.

Dedication

There are many companies and people that stand out in the ten year production of the *Sewhandy* sewing machine, i.e. STANDARD Sewing Machine Company of Cleveland, SINGER, Richard K. Hohmann, GENERAL ELECTRIC Corporation to name a few. However, one man stands above all the rest.

Volumes 1 and 2 are both dedicated to that one man: FREDERICK OSANN. He was the Founder and President of the FREDERICK OSANN Company of New York from 1907 until its purchase by SINGER in mid 1934.

He assisted the designer with improvements to the *Sewhandy*, and managed its marketing and production thru the STANDARD Sewing Machine Company of Cleveland.

FREDERICK OSANN became President of the STANDARD Sewing Machine Company of Cleveland in 1930 after STANDARD had financial difficulties. In spite of their financial problems, he was able to continue production of the well known STANDARD Sewing Machine product line.

Even after SINGER acquired his company and the *Sewhandy* in mid 1934, he continued development and research in the *Sewhandy* and other sewing machines thru his partnership with designer Richard K. Hohmann.

Table of Contents

THE FIRST *Sewhandy*

The *Sewhandy* design was the brainstorm of an independent inventor and designer named Richard K. Hohmann of New York City. On December 24, 1927, he filed for a patent on Sewing Machine (US Pat 1916860 – July 4, 1933).

Hohmann had a new and unique design. What he needed now was a sewing machine manufacturer. He contacted a nearby industrial sewing machine manufacturer, the FREDERICK OSANN Company of New York.

A contract between the FREDERICK OSANN Company and Richard Hohmann was worked out sometime prior to December 24, 1927.

The FREDERICK OSANN Company of New York is best known for their primary product, the Osann Fur Machine. They also manufactured and were agents for other makers machines.

The manufactured machines included Union Button Sewing and Union Ticket Sewing machines, Union Snap Fastener Machines, *Osann-Standard High Speed Stitching Machines*, Osann Buttonhole Machines, Osann Big Bobbin Machines, Osann Fur Beating Machines, and Osann Hat Leather Machines.

July 4, 1933.

R. K. HOHMANN

1,916,860

SEWING MACHINE

Filed Dec. 24, 1927

2 Sheets-Sheet 1

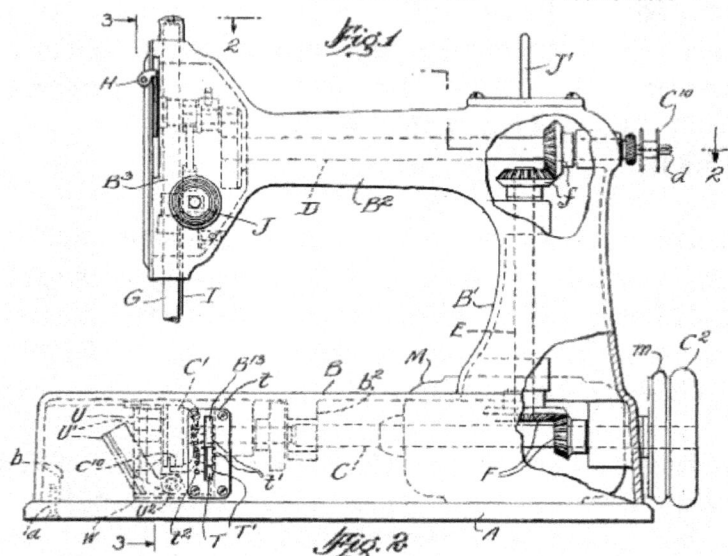

Fig. 1

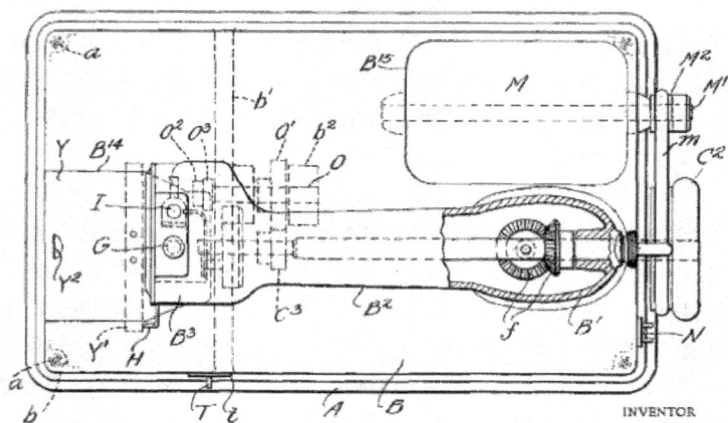

Fig. 2

INVENTOR

RICHARD K. HOHMANN

BY

John E. Hubbell

ATTORNEY

2

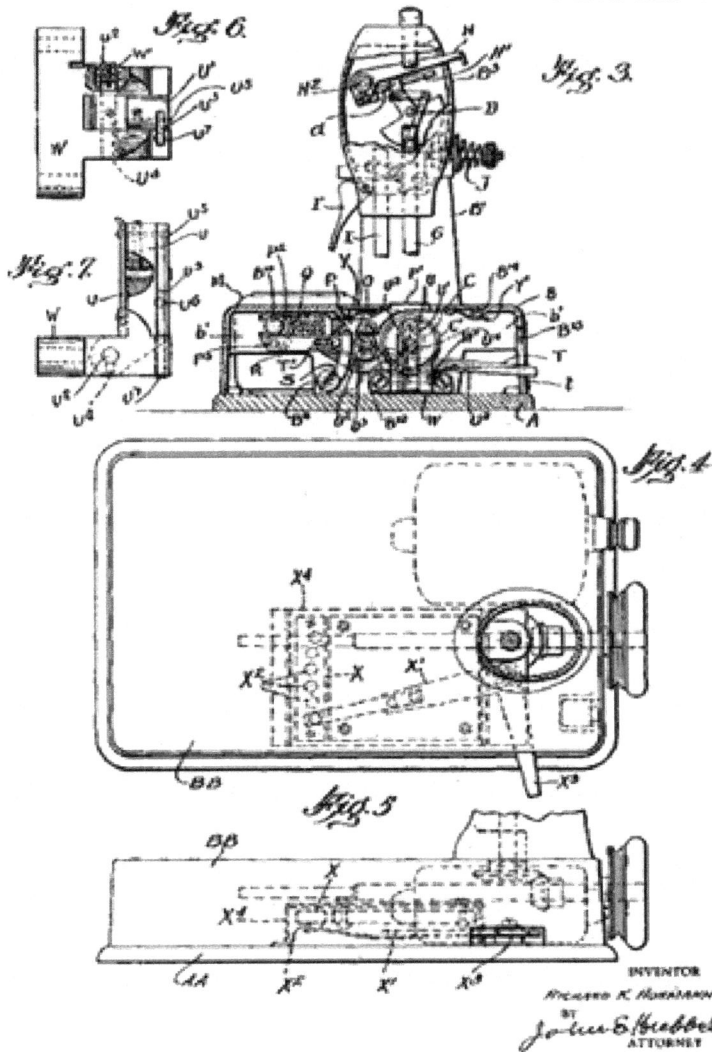

Fig. 6.

Fig. 7.

Fig. 3.

Fig. 4.

Fig. 5.

INVENTOR

Richard K. Hohmann

BY

John E. Hubbell

ATTORNEY

3

The **FREDERICK OSANN** Company assigned the actual manufacturing to the **STANDARD** Sewing Machine Company of Cleveland. The most likely reason for this is that **STANDARD** was well known with the women sewing at home. Their name was a household word, much like **SINGER** (though not that well known). In contrast, very few outside of the industrial sewing machine trade were aware of the **FREDERICK OSANN** Company.

The **STANDARD** Sewing Machine Company was located in Cleveland, Ohio. William S. Mack and his brother, Frank Mack, founded it in 1884. Under license from the **FREDERICK OSANN** Company, **STANDARD** began manufacturing the *Sewhandy* sewing machines around February 1928. At least the first 1,100 machines were labeled **STANDARD** on the sewing machine neck. Later models were all labeled with *Sewhandy*.

Something happened to **STANDARD** in late 1929. Maybe it was the Fall of the Stock Market. Maybe it was the beginning of the Great Depression. Government records indicate that by May 29, 1930, Frederick Osann was both the President of the **FREDERICK OSANN** Company and the **STANDARD** Sewing Machine Company (with all its assets and debts).

In June 1931, Frederick Osann and **STANDARD** contractually agreed to sell 5,000 *Sewhandy* machines to **GENERAL ELECTRIC** (GE). These 5,000 machines would bear the GE label (*MODEL*

A) and be sold thru the GE sales network. One of the more important parts of the arrangement was that it was agreed that no more machines (after the 750 currently in production) would be marketed as *Sewhandy* while GENERAL ELECTRIC was marketing their *MODEL A*. So it appears while the *Sewhandy* continued to be available after that, it was most likely labeled as a GENERAL ELECTRIC *MODEL A* and not a *Sewhandy*.

This coincides with my research that shows many *Sewhandy* newspaper ads in 1929 thru 1932, but none after that. On the flip side, GENERAL ELECTRIC *MODEL A* ads show-up beginning in 1932 and run thru mid 1935.

In mid 1934 the FREDERICK OSANN Company was sold to the SINGER Manufacturing Company for an undisclosed amount. SINGER immediately formed a "front" corporation called the OSANN Corporation to continue manufacturing the STANDARD sewing machine product line including the *Sewhandy*.

While SINGER did buy out the FREDERICK OSANN Company, none of the Osann Sewing Machines appear to have been produced later by SINGER. The SINGER website does not even mention any acquisition of the FREDERICK OSANN Company.

However, the records do show that SINGER continued using the "STANDARD Sewing Machine of Cleveland" name, and manufactured the STANDARD product line (including the *Sewhandy* under the successors to STANDARD label) until November 1938. At that time, SINGER dissolved the OSANN Corporation.

It does not appear that SINGER continued the exclusive marketing contract that had been arranged for the GENERAL ELECTRIC *MODEL A*, and for some period of time in 1934 thru 1935 both models (with different motors) may have been marketed under different labels at the same time.

All production of *Sewhandy* sewing machines ended by late 1938.

IDENTIFYING YOUR
Sewhandy

The *Sewhandy* (including GENERAL ELECTRIC *MODEL A*) was produced from February 1928 thru late 1938. It evolved and went thru numerous changes during its 10-year manufacturing run.

Some of the changes were extensive, but most of them were minor details such as labeling. Those changes allow us to estimate an approximate manufacturing date for each machine.

I have been unable to find a manufacturers listing of what serial number was assigned on what date. There were four different companies (Standard Sewing Machine Company of Cleveland, Frederick Osann Company of New York, The Osann Corporation Singer, and General Electric) involved in the manufacturing or marketing, and it appears that each had different serial numbers.

In this chapter, I will identify specific details on a *Sewhandy* for each period of time. If your machine has that feature, then it will fall into that period of time.

One exception.... The Face Plates were sometimes switched (just like on the SINGER 221) depending on owner preferences.

Place the front of the machine facing you. Look at the area of the machine bed top directly in front of the bottom of the vertical arm. Refer to the photos below.

Does your machine have the decal in front of the bottom of the arm in gold lettering?

DES. PAT. 80185
OTHER PATS. PENDING

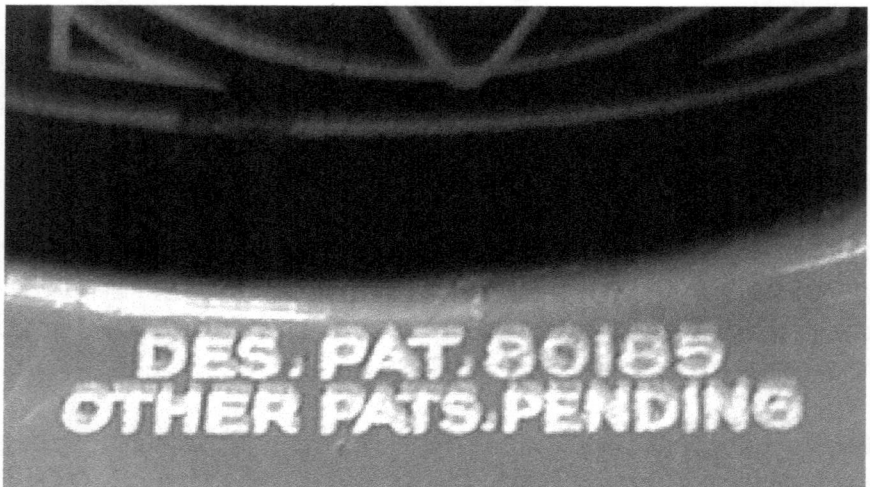

U. S. Design Patent 80185 was granted on December 29, 1929. *Sewhandy* machines made after this date, and all GE *MODEL A*'s, had this decal.

If your machine has this decal and it is a *Sewhandy*, go to page 21.

If your machine has this decal and it is a General Electric *Model A*, go to page 29.

If your machine does not have the DES. PAT. 80185 OTHER PATS. PENDING decal, it was made by prior to December 29, 1929. Continue on to page 11.

**STANDARD Sewing machine of
Cleveland *Sewhandy***

STANDARD *Sewhandy*

There are three variants of the STANDARD *Sewhandy.* The models break-down into the following groups:

1) STANDARD (Early) produced from the earliest production beginning in February thru August 1928.

2) *Sewhandy* (Mid) manufactured from August 1928 thru early 1929.

3) STANDARD *Sewhandy* (Late) made from early 1929 thru mid 1929.

All three variants share the same design features, with a few exceptions. These exceptions date the machine. All three share the following:

1) The machines have aluminum beds weighing 11¾ pounds.

2) They come in four colors: Green, Blue, Rose, and Black.

3) There is a winged STANDARD Sewing Machine Company logo in the center of the machine bed. There are two versions of the logo.

Early Decal (Cleveland, U.S.A. below logo)

Later Decal (Cleveland U.S.A. above logo)

4) The Slide Plate has a round hole.

5) This *Sewhandy* has a GE motor.

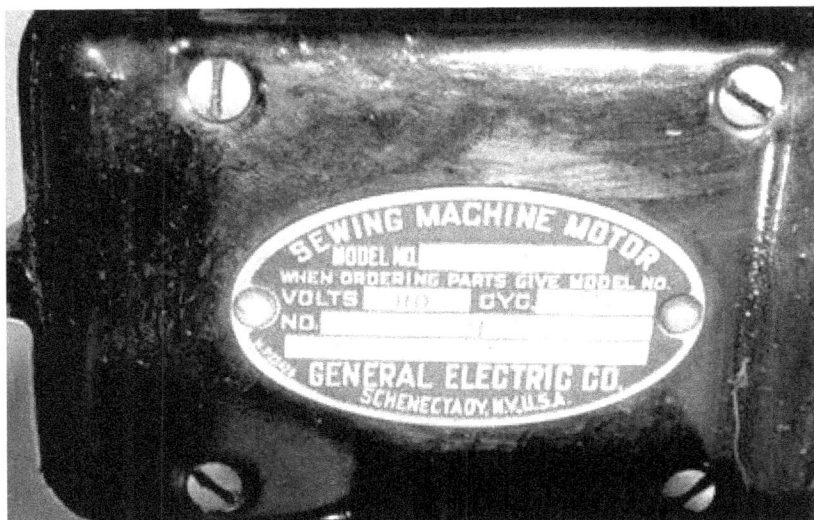

6) The Face Plate is plain chrome.

7) The serial number is on the right side of the Stitch Regulator Plate (starts with a "J-").

8) **All have the General Electric 75 Watt Lamp Shade and Socket Assembly with the long chrome end.**

On this unit, the brown switch has "GE" molded into the surface.

Which STANDARD do you have? Place the front of the machine facing you. Look at the neck of your *Sewhandy* and match the gold lettered decal with the one of the pictures on the following pages.

Earliest Production

The neck decal design below is found on STANDARD Sewing Machine of Cleveland machines from the earliest production from February thru August 1928. If yours reads *"Sewhandy"*, move on to "Mid Production" on the next page.

The earliest winged logos have "Cleveland, U.S.A." below the wings. These are on the STANDARD Sewing Machine of Cleveland machines from the earliest production from March thru August 1928. If yours has "Cleveland U.S.A." above the wings, move on to "Mid Production".

Mid Production

The neck decal design below is found on a STANDARD Sewing Machine of Cleveland *Sewhandy* from August 1928 thru early 1929. If yours reads "STANDARD *Sewhandy*", move on to "Late Production" below.

The Mid and Late Production logo on the bed is the same. It has Cleveland U.S.A. above the wings and is shown below.

Late Production

The neck decal design below is found on a **STANDARD** Sewing Machine of Cleveland machine from early to mid 1929. Note: If your *Sewhandy* has "STANDARD *Sewhandy*" with no bordering decal around it, then you have a later **OSANN** Corp **SINGER** version with a cast iron bed. Go to page 39.

Remember, all of the **STANDARD** *Sewhandy* sewing machines had aluminum beds with cast iron arms. If a magnet sticks to your bed, it is **NOT** a *Sewhandy* machine made by the **STANDARD** Sewing Machine Company, but is a later model from either the **FREDERICK OSANN** Company on page 21, or the **OSANN** Corp **SINGER** on page 39.

Note: It is not possible to tell where the last **STANDARD** *Sewhandy* model stops and the first **FREDERICK OSANN** Company *Sewhandy* begins. All we know is that it was sometime in mid 1929. This is when **FREDERICK OSANN** acquired and became President of the **STANDARD** Sewing Machine Company of Cleveland.

The original carrying case for all these models had two brass Eagle Lock of Terryville, Conn outer latches with a brass SOSY of New York center key latch marked "made in Germany" and "Pat Pending."

FREDERICK OSANN Company
Sewhandy

FREDERICK OSANN Company
Sewhandy

The next *Sewhandy* machines are those manufactured by the FREDERICK OSANN Company, a corporation of New York. Do not confuse this with the later OSANN Corporation - SINGER, a corporation of Pennsylvania.

These *Sewhandy* sewing machines were manufactured from mid 1929 until early 1932. Note: As written previously, it is not possible to tell where the last STANDARD *Sewhandy* model stops and the first FREDERICK OSANN Company *Sewhandy* begins.

Because of the marketing and distribution agreement with GE in June 1931, *Sewhandy* marketing ceased. All of the production beginning in early 1932 was labeled "GENERAL ELECTRIC (GE) *MODEL* A". This continued until SINGER acquired the FREDERICK OSANN Company in 1934.

The FREDERICK OSANN Company *Sewhandy* machines also had aluminum beds weighing 11 ¾ pounds.

Other details follow:

1) The machines came in four colors: Marine Blue, Larch Green, French Maroon, and Velvet Black.

2) There is a STANDARD Sewing Machine Company logo with Cleveland U.S.A. above the wings in the center of the machine bed.

3) The neck decal design below is found on all FREDERICK OSANN Company Sewhandy machines. Note: If your *Sewhandy* has "STANDARD *Sewhandy*" with no bordering decal around it, then you have a later OSANN Corp-SINGER version with a cast iron bed. Go to page 39.

4) All but the earliest of this model has the DES. PAT. 80185 decal.

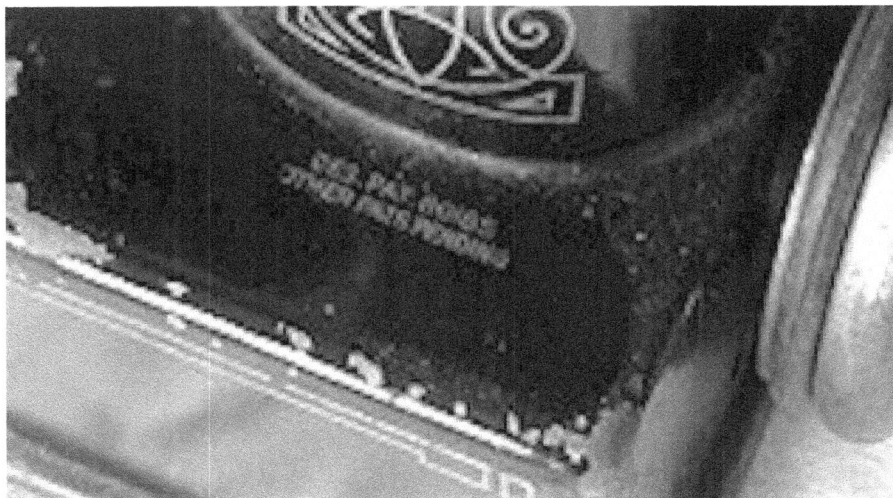

5) The Slide Plate has a round hole.

6) The early Face Plate is plain chrome. This is the same one that is used on the earlier STANDARD *Sewhandy* sewing machines.

7) The later models have the ornate floral urn scroll design on their Face Plate.

8) The serial number is on the right side of the Stitch Regulator Plate (starts with a "J-").

9) This *Sewhandy* also has the GE motor.

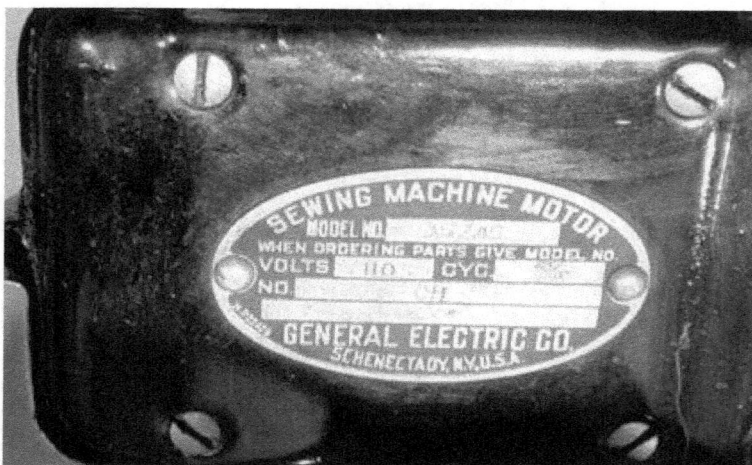

If your *Sewhandy* does not have the **GENERAL ELECTRIC** motor, but has an **OSANN CORP** motor, go to page 39.

10)   All have the General Electric 75 Watt Lamp Shade and Socket Assembly with the long chrome end.

On this unit, the brown switch has "GE" molded into the surface.

GENERAL ELECTRIC *MODEL A*

GENERAL ELECTRIC
MODEL A

The next *Sewhandy* machines are those distributed and sold by GENERAL ELECTRIC (GE). These machines were not labeled as *Sewhandy* machines, but were identified as the GENERAL ELECTRIC *MODEL A*. (Sewhandy production stopped in early 1932).

The *MODEL A*s were manufactured for GE from July 1931 until mid 1934 by the FREDERICK OSANN Corporation at the STANDARD Sewing Machine Company of Cleveland factory.

In mid 1934, SINGER bought out the FREDERICK OSANN Company, and subsequently formed a dummy corporation, the OSANN Corporation, to continue manufacturing the STANDARD Sewing Machine product line. From mid 1934 on for a couple of years, the OSANN Corporation SINGER manufactured the *MODEL A* for GE.

Like the later FREDERICK OSANN Company and all the OSANN Corporation (SINGER) *Sewhandy* machines, the GE *MODEL A* machines produced after mid 1932 had cast iron beds that increased their weight to 15¾ pounds. Some of the 11 ¾ pounds GE *MODEL A*s with aluminum beds should still exist, but they will be rare. Note: If a magnet sticks to yours, it is a cast iron *Model A.*

Other details follow:
  1) *MODEL A*s came in one color: Green.

2) The neck decal design below is found on all the **GENERAL ELECTRIC** *MODEL A* machines.

3) There is a GE logo in the center of the machine bed on the early *MODEL A*s, but the logo is gone on the later ones.

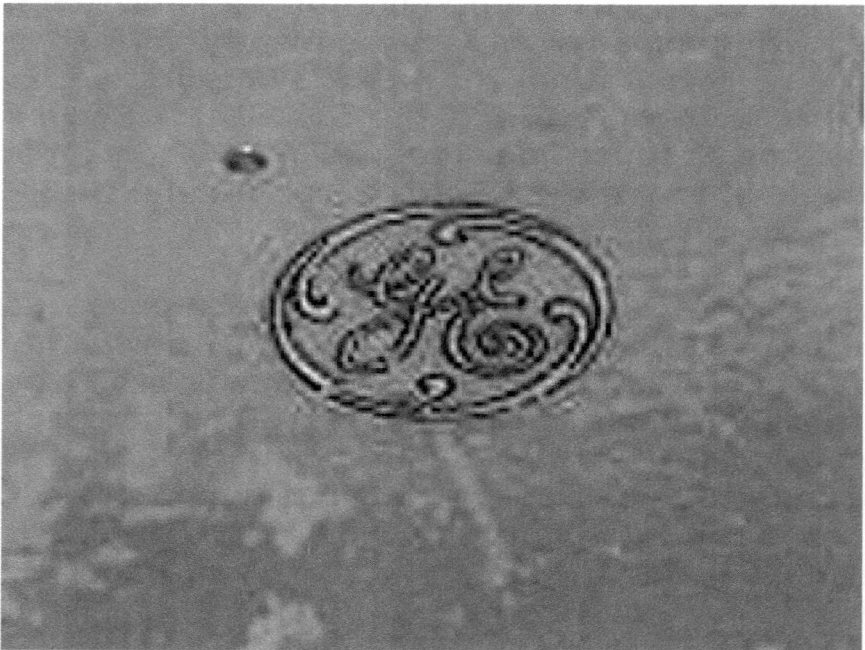

4) The DES. PAT. 80185 decal is on all GE *MODEL A* machines.

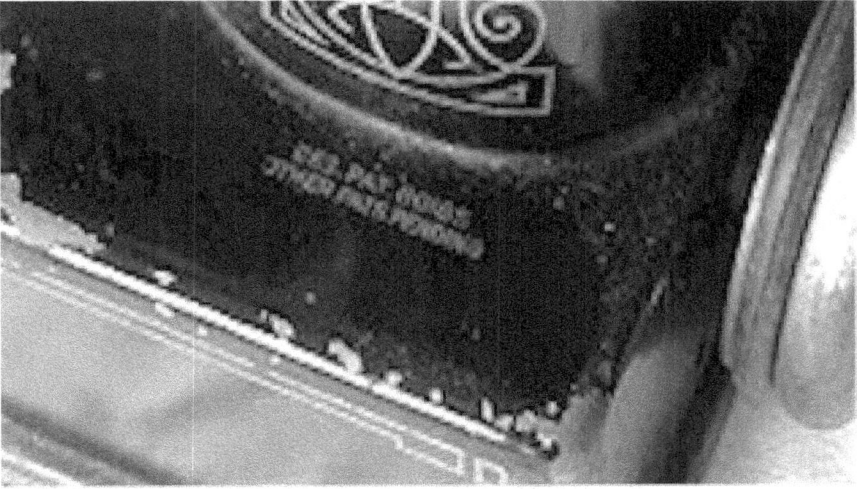

5) The Slide Plate has a round hole on the early models.

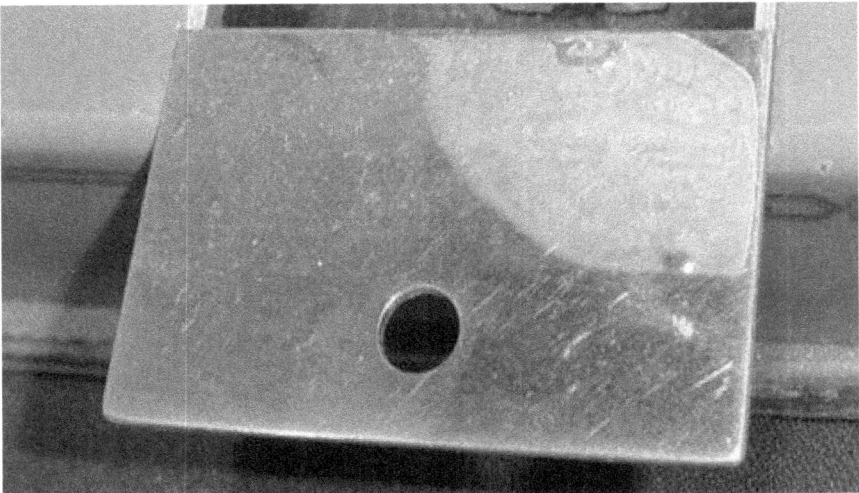

6) On the later _MODEL A_ machines, the Slide Plate has a grooved indent finger pull instead of a hole to pull it open.

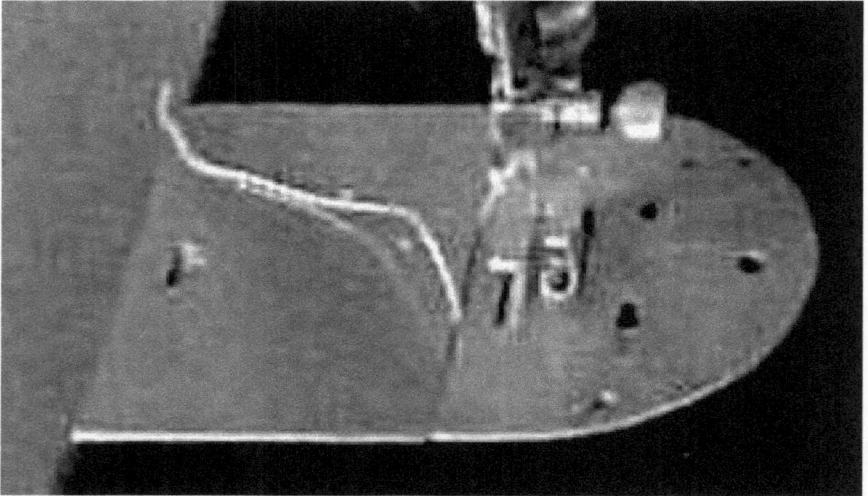

7) The _MODEL A_ has a GE motor.

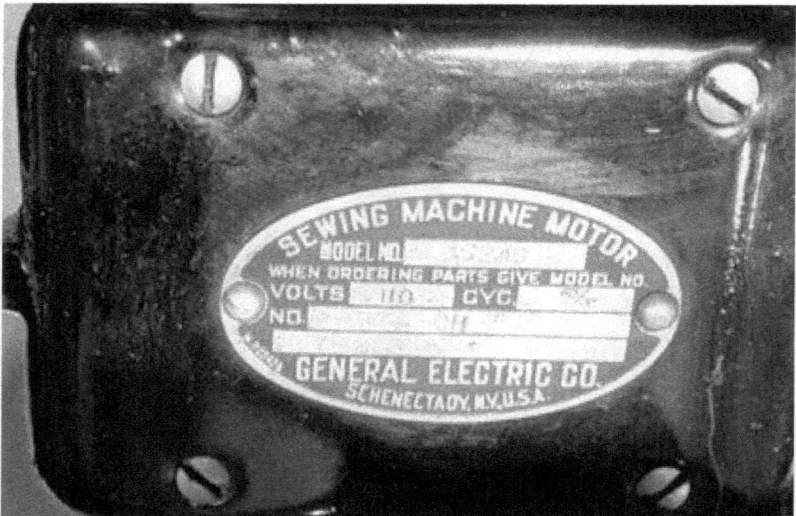

8) The Face Plate on the early *MODEL A* has the ornate floral urn scroll design.

9) The later models have the GE design on their Face Plate.

10) The serial number on the earlier *MODEL A* is on a plate on the rear of the machine. See the photo below.

11) The serial number on the later *MODEL A* is on a plate in the bobbin access well. See the photo below.

12) All have the General Electric 75-Watt Lamp Shade and Socket Assembly with the short chrome end. Compare this with the long chrome end on pages 15 and 27.

13) On this model, the brown switch has no markings. Compare this with the "GE" marked switch on page 15 and 27.

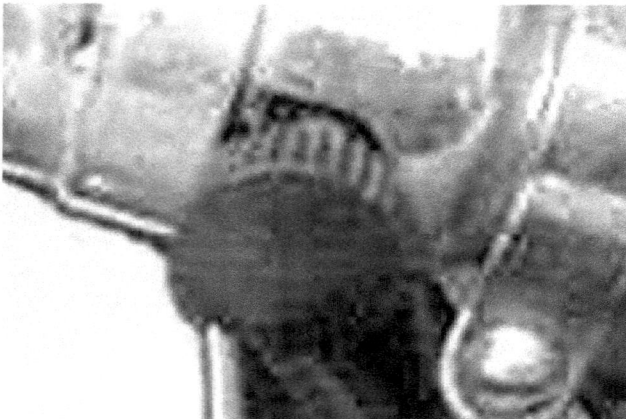

14) The *MODEL A* also has a 6 inch ruler decal on the front bed edge. This decal is unique to the **GENERAL ELECTRIC** *MODEL A.*

15) The *MODEL A* Stitch Regulator Plate does not have a Serial Number on it. Instead, it has the words "SHORT" – "STITCH" – "LONG" printed on its right side.

OSANN Corporation-SINGER
Sewhandy

OSANN Corporation-SINGER
Sewhandy

These are the newest of the *Sewhandy* machines. They were manufactured from mid 1934 until late 1938.

In mid 1934, SINGER bought out the FREDERICK OSANN Company and subsequently formed their dummy corporation, the OSANN Corporation, to continue manufacturing the *Sewhandy* machines along with the rest of the STANDARD Sewing Machine product line.

The OSANN Corporation – SINGER *Sewhandy* machines all have the cast iron beds making these models weigh 15¾ pounds. These models came in one color: Black.

The easiest way to tell if you have an OSSAN - SINGER *Sewhandy* made from mid 1934 to the end of production in late 1938 is to look for the label on the front bed edge. An OSSAN - SINGER *Sewhandy* will have the decal reading:

MANUFACTURED BY
THE OSANN CORPORATION
NEW YORK, N.Y.
SUCCESSORS TO
THE STANDARD
SEWING MACHINE COMPANY

See the actual decal on the next page.

MANUFACTURED BY
THE OSANN CORPORATION
NEW YORK, N.Y.
SUCCESSORS TO
THE STANDARD
SEWING MACHINE COMPANY

Remember, this is the OSANN Corporation that SINGER formed as their dummy corporation after they bought out the FREDERICK OSANN Company. It was based out of the SINGER headquarters in New York City with its manufacturing office in the SINGER plant at Elizabethport, NJ. This is not the FREDERICK OSANN Company that originally worked with the STANDARD Sewing Machine Company of Cleveland to produce the first *Sewhandy* machines.

You can also tell the model by looking at the motor or motor plate. Machines made prior to SINGER taking over used the GENERAL ELECTRIC motor. As soon as SINGER formed their OSANN Corporation, they mounted a OSANN Corporation label plate over an unlabeled SINGER BRK/BUK series motor. See the example on the next page.

SEWING MACHINE MOTOR
CAT. NO. 05
VOLTS 110
CYCLES 25 TO 75 & D.C.
WATTS 50
THE OSANN CORPORATION
NEW YORK, N.Y.

The **OSANN** Corporation – **SINGER** *Sewhandy* machine labeling or decals are much simpler. The winged **STANDARD** Sewing Machine Company logo in the center of the machine bed was eliminated.

The neck label still read Standard *Sewhandy*, but the lettering was changed and the gold borders were eliminated.

STANDARD
Sewhandy

Other details follow:

1) The Face Plate has the same ornate floral urn scroll design used on the FREDERICK OSANN Company *Sewhandy*.

16) **All have the General Electric 75 Watt Lamp Shade and Socket Assembly with the short chrome end. Compare this with the long chrome end on pages 15 and 27.**

17) **On this model, the brown switch has no markings. Compare this with the "GE" marked switch on page 15 and 27.**

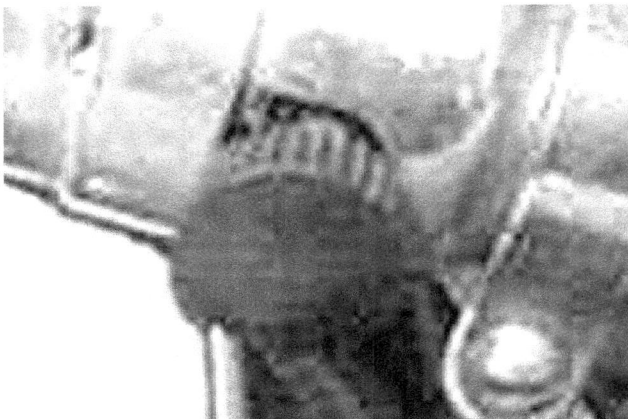

18) The Slide Plate has a grooved indent finger pull instead of a hole to pull it open.

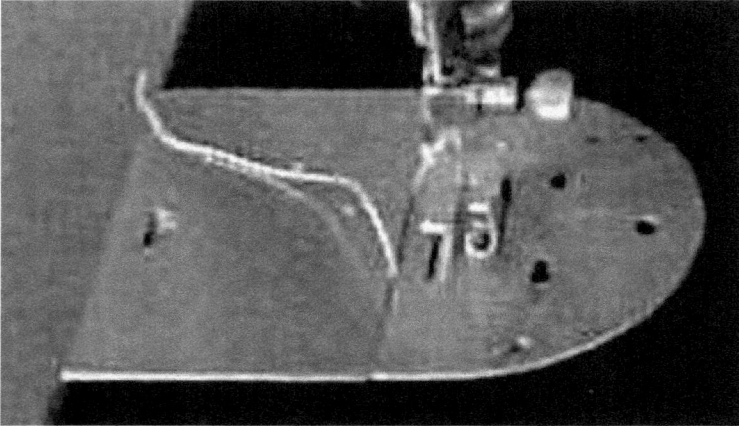

19) The serial number is on the right side of the Stitch Regulator Plate (starts with a "J-").

There are not any other differences thru the end of production in late 1938.

Model Specifications

STANDARD Sewing Machine Company *Sewhandy*

Made in Cleveland
Manufacturing Period: Feb 1928 thru Mid 1929
General Electric (GE) Motor
4 Colors: Green, Blue, Rose, and Black
Black or Tan Carrying Case
Aluminum beds making weight 11¾ lbs
Early Center Bed Decal – Cleveland USA above
Late Center Bed Decal – Cleveland USA below
Plain Chrome Face Plate
Slide Plate finger hole
No DES. PAT. 80185 on right front bed
Standard neck decal – gold borders (Early)
Sewhandy neck decal – gold borders (Mid)
STANDARD *Sewhandy* neck decal – gold borders (Late)
SN on front stitch length lever plate
Long GE Lamp Shade and Socket Assembly
"GE" marking on Lamp Shade switch
Case outside latches Eagle Lock
Center latch SOSY Pat Pending

Model Specifications

FREDERICK OSANN Company
Sewhandy

Made in Cleveland
Manufacturing Period: Mid 1929 thru Early 1932
General Electric (GE) Motor
4 Colors: Larch Green, Marine Blue, French Maroon, Velvet Black
Black or Tan Carrying Case
Aluminum beds weight 11¾ lbs
Center Bed Decal – Cleveland USA below
Plain Chrome Face Plate (Early)
Scroll Chrome Face Plate (Late)
Slide Plate finger hole
No DES. PAT. 80185 on right front bed (Earliest)
DES. PAT. 80185 on right front bed (Later)
STANDARD *Sewhandy* neck decal – gold borders
SN on front stitch length lever plate
Long GE Lamp Shade and Socket Assembly
"GE" marking on Lamp Shade switch
Case outside latches Eagle Lock
Center latch SOSY Pat Pending

Model Specifications

GENERAL ELECTRIC
MODEL A

Made in Cleveland (Early)
Made in Elizabethport, New Jersey (Later)
Manufacturing Period: July 1931 thru Mid 1934
Mid 1934 to around 1936 (SINGER)
General Electric (GE) Motor
Colors: Green
Aluminum beds 11¾ lbs to Mid 1932
Cast Iron beds 15¾ lbs after Mid 1932
"GE" Center Bed Decal (Early)
No "GE" Center Bed Decal (Late)
Scroll Chrome Face Plate (Early)
"GE" Face Plate (Late)
Slide Plate has finger groove indentation
DES. PAT. 80185 on right front bed
General Electric neck decal – no borders
STITCH on front stitch length lever plate
SN on plate in bobbin bed area (Early)
SN on rear plate below motor (Late)
6 inch rule decal on right front bed edge
Short GE Lamp Shade and Socket Assembly
No markings on Lamp Shade switch
Case outside latches Langenau Cleveland
Center latch SOSY Pat 1717930 (July 1929)

Model Specifications

OSANN Corporation SINGER
Sewhandy

Made in Elizabethport, New Jersey
Manufacturing Period: Mid 1934 thru late 1938
SINGER BRK/BUK Motor
Colors: Black
Cast Iron beds 15¾ lbs
Scroll Chrome Face Plate
Slide Plate finger groove indentation
DES. PAT. 80185 on right front bed
Standard *Sewhandy* neck decal – <u>no borders</u>
OSANN Corp "Successor" decal on front bed
SN on front stitch length lever plate
Short GE Lamp Shade and Socket Assembly
No markings on Lamp Shade switch
Case outside latches Langenau Cleveland
Center latch SOSY Pat 1717930 (July 1929)

OPERATING
INSTRUCTIONS

This chapter is for those of you that did not get the Operating Instructions with your _Sewhandy._

Read These Valuable Suggestions
Regarding Your New *"Sewhandy"*
Sewing Machine

You now possess one of the most modern Electric Sewing Machines ever designed for home sewing.

In order that you may obtain the utmost enjoyment and service from your "Sew-handy," these suggestions and instructions have been carefully prepared especially for your use.

This booklet tells, in plain, easily understood language, how to get best results from your "Sewhandy." Study this booklet and you will find fascinating pleasure in learning all about the marvelous things your "Sewhandy" will do, and how easy it is to use and enjoy. Should you require any further information, feel free to write us.

THE
Standard Sewing Machine Co.
CLEVELAND, OHIO
U. S. A.

1

How to Remove the Machine and Replace it in the Carrying Case

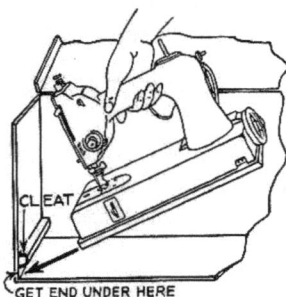

CLEAT

GET END UNDER HERE

FIRST remove the tray which contains the attachments, etc., tip the right end of the machine upward as shown in the above cut, and it will then lift out easily. To replace the machine in the case, tip the left end downward as shown, so that the end of the baseboard will fit into the recess under the cleat across the bottom of the case, as indicated by the arrow.

When packing the machine for traveling, be sure to place the piece of corrugated paper around the spool pin and between the spool plate and the underside of the tray, so that the machine will be held down securely by the latter when the lid of the case is closed.

Always keep the rheostat, when not in use, in the cloth bag prepared for it and place it on the bed of the machine under the arm, when putting the machine back into the case, to avoid scratching the enamel.

To Connect the Machine With Electric Current

TWO pieces of connection cord are packed with each machine. One of these cords has attached to it the foot control, or rheostat. Place the rheostat on the floor and plug the other end of the cord into the opening marked "Q" (Fig. 1), page 4. The other current supply cord has a flat plug on one end and a round plug on the other. Insert the flat plug into the opening in the bed of the machine marked "current connection," (Fig. 2), page 5. The other end of this wire has the round combination plug which can be screwed into any electric light socket or may be inserted into a floor or baseboard electric current outlet by pulling the screw part of the plug off, and inserting the two prongs of the plug into the outlet.

When you have finished sewing, always disconnect the supply cord from the house electric outlet and also from the machine.

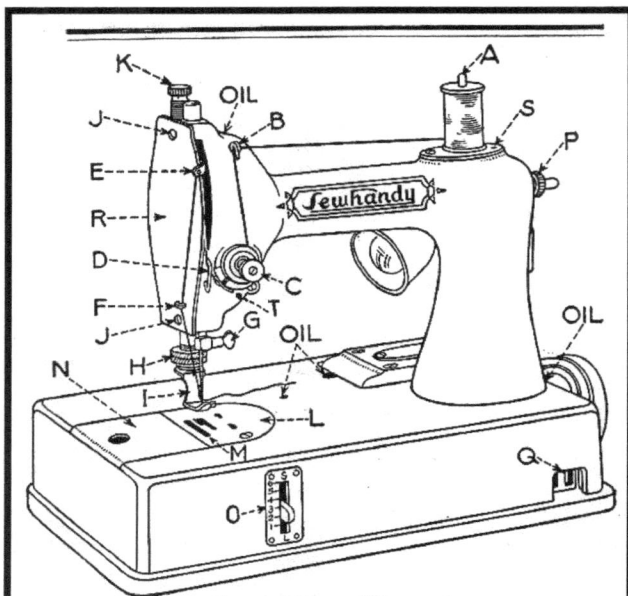

Front View—Figure 1

A   Spool Pin
B   Thread Guide
C   Tension
D   Thread Guide
E   Take-up
F   Thread Guide
G   Needle Clamp Screw
H   Presser Foot Nut
I   Presser Foot
J   Face Plate Screws
K   Presser Bar Cap Screw
L   Needle Plate
M   Feed
N   Slide Plate
O   Stitch Regulator
P   Bobbin Winder
Q   Foot Control Connection
R   Face Plate
S   Top Arm Cover
T   Spring Take-up

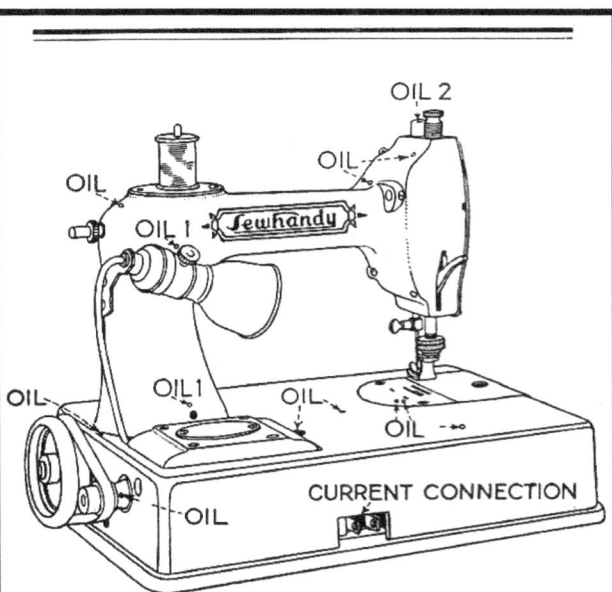

Rear View—Figure 2

Oiling Instructions

CAUTION! Use only the best light sewing machine oil, which can be purchased from the store or dealer where you obtained your "SEWHANDY" machine.

Oil moving parts frequently, as shown by oiling places indicated plainly on Fig. 2. All oiling places are easy to get at without removing the base of the machine.

In oiling through holes marked "Oil 1," Fig. 2, push the spout of the oil can all the way in against the shaft. *This is important.*

To oil the needle bar connection and the lower needle bar bearing, it will be necessary to remove the bottom screw "J" on the face plate "R" (Fig. 1) and loosen the

5

top screw, also "J," so that the face plate can be swung out of the way as shown in Fig. 3, to permit oiling these parts. The upper needle bar bearing is oiled through the hole marked "Oil 2," Fig. 2.

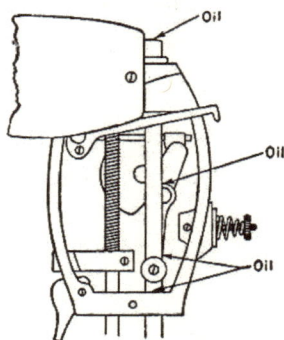

Figure 3

Use only a *few drops* of oil on each of these parts as, if too much oil is used, the surplus will be likely to drip on to and stain the fabric being stitched.

To oil the hook, take the bobbin case out and *put a drop or two of oil on the bobbin case bearing* surface of the hook. This should be done each time you start to use the machine, and if the machine is run steadily all day, should be done two or three times during that time. After this oiling, sew a minute or two on a piece of waste goods to absorb any surplus oil that may be on the hook.

Do not oil the gears. These are lubricated with a special grease at the factory and should not need attention for at least a year, and when they do, ordinary vaseline may be used.

Method of Threading the Spool Thread

THE correct method of threading is very simple, as shown by front view (Fig. 1). Place the spool on the spool pin "A," loop the thread into the guide "B," then down to the right of and between the tension discs "C," then into the loop of the spring take-up "T," then the guide "D" and up and through the take-up "E," then down through the thread guide "F" and thread through the eye of the needle from left to right.

To Remove the Bobbin Case

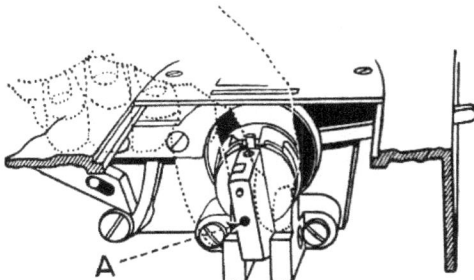

Figure 4

TURN the machine by hand until the take-up "E" (Fig. 1) is at its highest point. Raise the presser foot, remove any fabric you may have in the machine and cut the threads loose from the same. Pull the slide plate "N" (Fig. 1) to the left. This will provide sufficient opening in which to insert the thumb and forefinger of the left hand. Press the retaining latch "A" (Fig. 4) with the finger until the bobbin case retainer "B" (Fig. 5) falls back and then lift the bobbin case out, as shown in that figure.

7

To Remove the Bobbin from the Case

THROUGH the two large semi-circular openings "C" (Fig. 5) in the front of the bobbin case, press out the bobbin until you can grasp the rim with the thumb and finger and pull it out.

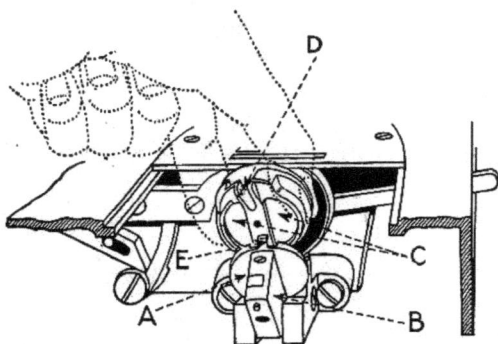

Figure 5

To Wind the Bobbin (See Fig. 6)

RAISE the presser foot "I" (Fig. 1) and see that the bobbin case is out of the machine, then place the bobbin on the winder "P" (Fig. 1) as shown in Fig. 6. Now draw some thread from the spool and wind the end around the bobbin three or four times by hand toward you, then hold the thread with the forefinger and keep a gentle pressure on it with the thumb, as shown in Fig. 6. Now start the machine with the foot as in sewing and run at a moderate speed until the bobbin is wound, not quite full. Never wind the bobbin full, as the thread is liable to slip off the rim and break in sewing.

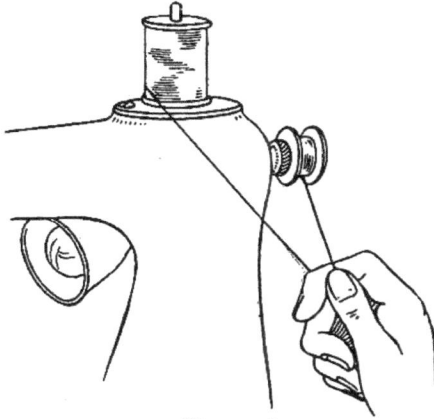

Figure 6

To Insert the Bobbin in the Case

PLACE the hole in the bobbin over the stem of the bobbin case and press it down into the case until the rim is below the edge of the case and the bobbin turns freely.

CAUTION! Always put the bobbin in the bobbin case so the thread will unwind in the direction of the arrow (Fig. 7).

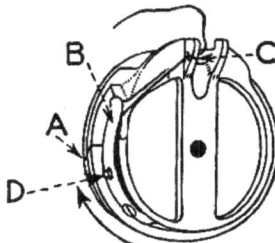

Figure 7

9

To Thread the Bobbin Case
(See Fig. 7)

WITH the bobbin inserted in the case so that the thread will unwind in the direction of the arrow as instructed, draw the thread through the slit "A," then under the tension spring "B" and thread through the hole "C." Now test the strength of the tension as per instructions for regulating the bobbin case tension. See page 11.

To Replace the Bobbin Case in the Machine

BE SURE to have the take-up and needle bar at their high position, then lay the bobbin case against the plate "A" (Fig. 5) with its forked part "D" (Fig. 5) over the holding tongue "E" of the plate "A," and close the latch "B" until it is firmly locked in place. If the latch will not lock securely you may be sure the bobbin case is not in its proper position.

CAUTION! The machine should never be started or run with the bobbin case in place until the latch is closed and securely locked.

Tensions

Perfect stitching depends largely upon the thread being drawn evenly into the fabric so it will look alike on both sides as shown in Fig. 8. To secure the proper tension do the following:

10

Figure 8

Figure 9

Figure 10

First—Regulate the Bobbin Tension.

Take hold of thread (Fig. 7) and pull out about six inches. Hold case suspended by thread. If case slips down, adjustment is too loose. Use small screw driver and adjust screw "D" (Fig. 7) slightly until the case will sustain itself when held still, but when jiggled a little, will gradually slide down the thread. This is the proper bobbin case tension adjustment, and it is rarely necessary to change it after it has been properly adjusted.

Second—Regulate Top Tension.

Turn the regulating nut "C" (Fig. 1) to the right to tighten and to the left to loosen this tension.

Sew on a piece of cloth and examine stitch. If the thread is straight along under side of fabric as in Fig. 9 then tighten the top tension "C" (Fig. 1) until stitch is the same on both sides of the fabric as shown in Fig. 8.

If the thread is straight along the top of fabric (Fig. 10), then loosen top tension slightly until stitch is the same on both sides of fabric as shown in Fig. 8.

11

To Regulate the Pressure Foot

TO regulate the pressure of the Presser Foot on the goods, adjust Presser Bar Cap Screw "K" (Fig. 1.) Turning this screw to the right will increase the pressure and to the left will lessen the pressure. The pressure should never be more than enough to feed the goods evenly. Light goods require less and heavy goods more pressure.

Stitch Regulation

THE length of the stitch is regulated by the stitch regulator "O" (Fig. 1). Move it up to shorten, and down to lengthen the stitch.

An Exclusive *"Sewhandy"* Feature

THE "Sewhandy" Machine cannot clog. Its improved round bobbin and open hook mechanism preclude the possibility of this common cause of complaint. Any accumulation of thread or lint can be removed quickly and easily.

To Set the Needle

TO INSERT and adjust the needle; first, be sure the needle is *straight* and has a *sharp point*. Turn the machine by hand until the needle bar is at its highest point. Hold the needle in the left hand with the flat side toward the right and loosen the needle clamp screw "G" (Fig. 1). Insert needle as far as possible. Now, tighten the clamp screw "G" down solid on the needle and test its security by trying to pull the needle out of the bar, which you should not be able to do.

CAUTION! It is very important that the needle be pushed up as far as it will go into the bar and that it be securely held with the clamp screw against the danger of coming out and breaking and injuring the sewing mechanism, in operation.

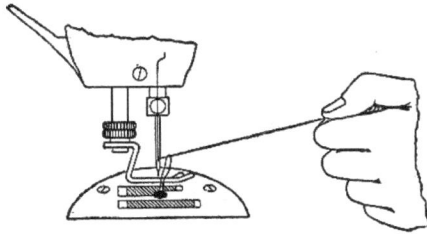

Fig. 11

To Prepare for Sewing

BEING sure that machine is threaded according to instructions, hold the end of the needle thread with the left hand, leaving it slack from the hand to the

13

needle. Turn the hand wheel away from you until the needle moves down and up again to its highest point. Then pull the needle thread taut and the bobbin thread will be drawn up through the needle hole in the plate as shown in Fig. 11. Lay both threads back under the presser foot and close the slide plate "N" (Fig. 1). Place the fabric under the presser foot, lower the same and you are ready to sew.

Operation

START the machine by pressing the foot on the rheostat. Should the machine fail to start because of heavy material or thick seams, keep the foot on the rheostat and at the same time give the hand wheel a slight turn away from you.

Speed

THE speed of the machine is very easily controlled by the pressure of the foot on the rheostat. More pressure giving greater speed, less pressure giving less speed.

Needles and Threads

IN SELECTING the thread and needle for the fabric to be sewed, refer to the following Table:

Material	Thread	Needle
Crepe, Georgette and Light Silk	90–100 Cotton O Silk	#11
Muslin, Cotton Goods, Medium Weight Silk and Linen	60–80 Cotton A-B Silk	#14
Heavy Cotton, Linen, Light Woolen, Heavy Silk	40–60 Cotton C Silk	#16
Heavy Woolens, Clothing, Coats, etc.	30–40 Cotton D Silk	#18

Best results are obtained with the best soft finished cotton and a good grade of sewing silk.

CAUTION! Be sure the needle to be used is straight and has a sharp point.

BE SURE TO USE ONLY GENUINE

Sewhandy

N E E D L E S

15

Helpful Suggestions

IF THE top thread breaks, examine the needle to make sure it is not bent and that it has a perfectly sharp point; also be sure it is set up as far as it will go into the needle bar and securely tightened with the needle clamp screw "G" (Fig. 1). Or the machine may not be properly threaded: See threading instructions page 7. Or your tension may be too tight or the thread too large for the size of the needle: See table for needle and thread sizes on page 15.

If the machine skips stiches it is most likely caused by a bent or imperfect point needle or because the needle is not set fully up in the needle bar.

Needle breakage is usually caused by the presser foot or attachment not being securely fastened with the presser foot nut "H" (Fig. 1), or because point of the needle is damaged or by pulling the work while sewing.

If the machine runs heavy use a few drops of kerosene in the various oil holes and after running it a few minutes oil with good light sewing machine oil.

Attachments

The attachments are the best obtainable and if used carefully and according to directions, satisfactory work will result.

Directions for Use of Attachments

HEMMING

RAISE the presser foot and needle bar; attach the hemmer in place of the presser foot (see cut). Insert the edge of the cloth in the hemmer, folded as shown; draw the cloth far enough through the hemmer so the needle will enter its extreme edge. Let the hemmer foot down and proceed to sew, guiding the work and keeping the scroll of the hemmer just full.

Any width of hem can be made with the hemmer and feller, by folding the goods the desired width of hem and passing the edge through as in narrow hemming.

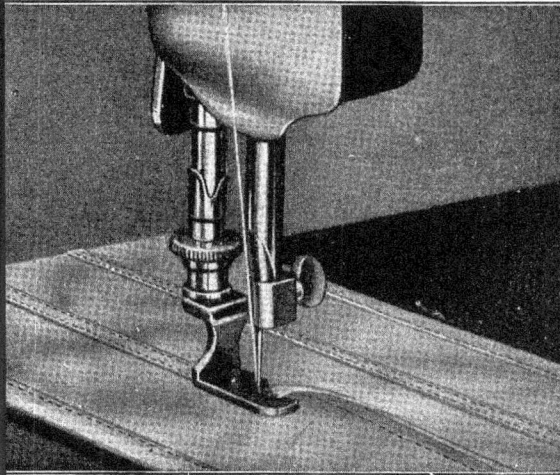

Hemming and Felling

17

Hemming and Felling

The hemmer is also the feller. Stitch two pieces together, their edges to the right, and the lower edge projecting about ¼ inch beyond the upper, then open the work out flat edges up; draw the edges at the beginning of the seam into the hemmer, and proceed to sew, as in cut on page 17. French seams suitable for curve or body seams can also be made with the feller by inserting two pieces with edges even.

Hemming and Sewing on Lace

The hemmer and feller which accompanies this machine is made with a slot for the needle to pass through instead of a round hole. This slot is to enable the operator to make a hem and sew on lace at the same time. Start a narrow hem and pass the end of the lace through the slot in the side of the hemmer, carrying it under the back

Hemming and Sewing On Lace, One Operation

of the hemmer and on top of the hem, as in cut on page 18; then proceed as in ordinary hemming. Keep the lace well in the slot so that the needle will catch it every time.

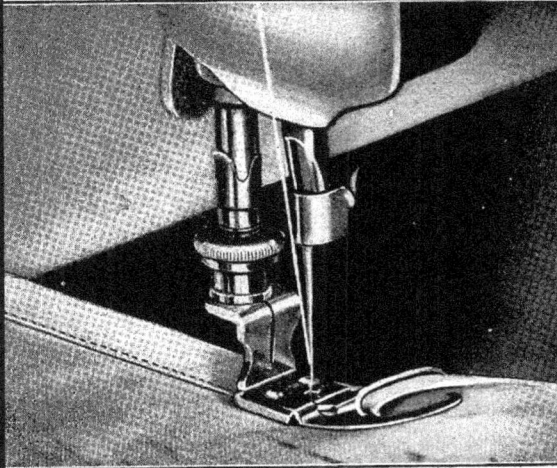

Wide Hemming

Wide Hemming

THE wide hemmers belong to the regular set of attachments, and are used for wide hemming and on heavy goods. Attach in place of presser foot. Fold the goods (by hand) the width of hem required, turning one fold only, adding about one-eighth of an inch, which will be turned under by the hemmer; introduce the edge of the cloth the same as for a narrow hem, and proceed in the same way, holding the goods in the right hand.

19

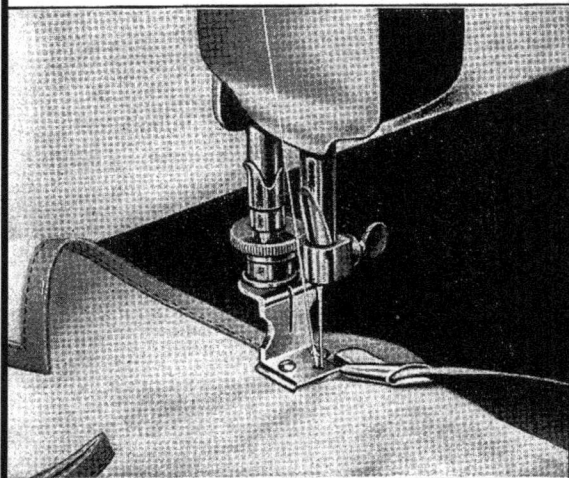
Binding

Binding

RAISE the presser bar and the needle. Attach the binder in place of the presser foot.

Pass the binding through the scroll of the binder and draw it back under the needle. Place the edge of the goods to be bound between the scrolls of the binder and draw it under the needle. Lower the presser bar and sew as usual.

For bias binding, goods of any description can be used. For the binder ordinarily used, the binding should be cut seven-eighths of an inch wide, in order to turn under at the edges.

To Bind With Common Dress Braid

PROCEED the same as when using bias binding, as explained above. The only difference is, the dress braid being narrower, the edges will not be turned under, as is the case with bias binding.

To Bind Scallops

IN BINDING scallops, after binding around the scallops, stop the machine with the needle in the goods, fold the elbow or angle of the following scallop so as to form as nearly as possible a straight line, and continue binding. Hold the goods being bound, a little firmer than the binding, which will prevent its being drawn.

To Make French Folds

ATTACH the binder as usual. Pass the binding through the binder and sew as usual, stitching the edges together. This can be sewed on at the same time if desired.

TUCKING
To Attach Tucker to Machine

ATTACH the tucker firmly to the presser bar in place of the foot; see that the lever which works the creasing arm is under the needle clamp screw.

To Adjust the Tucker

LOOSEN the thumb-screw. The *width of the tuck* is regulated by the distance of the edge-guide to the right of the line of the needle or seam; the tuck will be exactly as wide as this distance. *The space between tucks* is determined by the distance of the

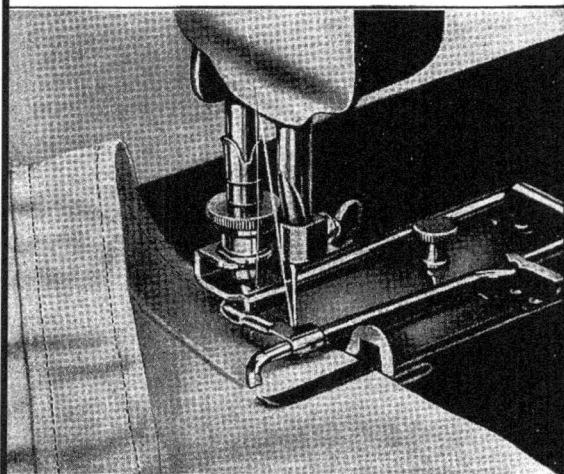

Tucking

creasing blade to the left of the line of the needle or seam.

The figures on the scales on the tucker are for convenience in adjusting the width of tuck and distance between tucks. If the guides on the two scales are at the same figure (to the right), then the creasing blade is twice the distance to the left of the needle that the edge-guide is to the right, and the tucks will meet; that is, the crease of one tuck will lie exactly over the seam of the last tuck. When adjusted as wanted, tighten thumb-screw.

To Operate Tucker

MAKE the first crease in the usual manner by hand. Insert the cloth between the creasing arm and blade and the blade spring; the part that is to be tucked on the top. Draw it to the right until the crease of the cloth comes against the edge-guide. Then sew as in plain work. Fold at the crease in making subsequent tucks. Take care that the tuck last made is inside the gauge that is directly beneath the creaser blade.

RUFFLING

To Attach the Ruffler

RAISE the presser bar and needle, remove the presser foot and put the ruffler in its place, adjust so that the needle passes through the center of the hole in the foot, and the prongs of the fork will be on either side of the needle clamp. Fasten firmly in place. Use an occasional drop of oil on the fork lever hinge.

71

Plain Ruffling

To Operate Ruffler

INSERT the goods to be ruffled between the blued blades, pushing the cloth from you with the aid of the small screw-driver or stiletto, until it lies smoothly under the needle, over first but under second guide. Drop the presser bar and proceed as in plain sewing. To make a very full ruffle, shorten the stitch and turn the thumb-screw or disc to the left until you have the desired amount of fullness. To make wide plaits, turn thumb-screw to the left until it stops, then lengthen the stitch to match; the length of stitch should be regulated so that the plaits will lie evenly and not pile upon each other, or lie too far

24

apart. To make fine scant gathers, use short stitch and regulate ruffller by turning thumb-screw or disc to the right until the blued blade moves back enough to just catch the goods, thus making the finest possible ruffle.

Ruffling and Sewing On

PLACE goods below both blued blades on feed of machine and up over first guide. Place material to be ruffled as in "plain ruffling," under second guide. Proceed as in plain sewing, being careful to keep the goods smooth and straight.

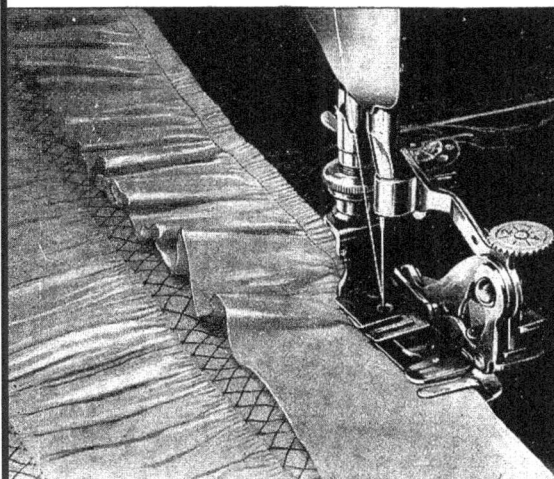

Ruffling and Sewing On

Sewing On Ruffle With Narrow Heading

FOLD over edge to be gathered ½ inch. Place material to be ruffled between blued blades, under second guide and over first guide. Place garment underneath the ruffler, allowing it to come to the left of the needle the width of the ruffle; this will make bottom of ruffle and bottom of garment perfectly even. Be sure to keep garment straight.

Ruffling, Sewing On and Putting On Facing at One Stitching Operation

PLACE goods and material to be ruffled exactly as in "ruffling and sewing on." Place facing over the blued blades and under the foot, and proceed as usual, being careful to keep goods and facing straight and smooth.

Underbraiding

Underbraider

USE the short prong braider foot in place of the regular presser foot. The underbraider is placed in position as follows: At the right of the presser foot you will see two openings. Place the point A in the opening farthest from you, and the pin C in the opening nearest you. Push the attachment into these openings as far as it will go, which will fasten it. Before pushing it into place be careful to put the braid into the channel of the attachment with enough projecting from the end to insure its coming under the needle and presser foot. Place the goods wrong side up with the pattern traced on the upper side, and proceed as in ordinary sewing, following the pattern.

Underbraiding

27

Sewhandy

Portable Electric Family Sewing Machine
PARTS LIST

Part No.	Name
9000	Arm
9001	Arm Screw (3 used)
9026	Arm Dowels (2 used)
9003-A	Arm Cover Plate (Assem.)
9006	Arm Cover Plate Screw
9015	Arm Shaft (Top)
9024	Arm Shaft Miter Gear
9017	Arm Shaft Gear Set Screw (2 used)
9018	Arm Shaft Collar
9019	Arm Shaft Collar Set Screw
9020	Arm Shaft (Vertical)
9021	Arm Shaft Vertical Bushing (Upper)
9022	Arm Shaft Vertical Bushing (Lower)
9028	Arm Shaft Vertical Bushing Set Screw (2 used)
9024	Arm Shaft Vertical Miter Gear (Upper)
9017	Arm Shaft Vertical Miter Gear Screw (2 used)
9025	Arm Shaft Vertical Bevel Gear (Lower)
9026	Arm Shaft Vertical Bevel Gear Pin
9027-A	Arm Shaft Vertical Assembled with Gear and Pin
9040	Bed
9041	Bed Base
9042	Bed Base Screw (5 used)
9043	Bed Pads (Rubber) (4 used)
9044	Belt Wheel
9019	Belt Wheel Set Screw (2 used)
9045	Bobbin
9046	Bobbin Winder
9047	Bobbin Case
9048	Bobbin Case Tension Spring
9049	Bobbin Case Tension Spring Screw (Holding)
9050	Bobbin Case Tension Spring Screw (Adjusting)
9051	Bobbin Case Bobbin Retaining Spring
102-C	Bobbin Case Bobbin Retaining Spring Screw

28

PARTS LIST

Part No.	Name
9053-A	Bobbin Case, (Assem.)
9069-B	Bobbin Case Retainer
9055-B	Bobbin Case Retainer Bracket
9056	Bobbin Case Retainer Bracket Screw (2 used)
9075-AB	Bobbin Case Retainer Plate (Assem.)
9076	Bobbin Case Retainer Plate Stud Set Screw
9061	Bobbin Case Retainer Fulcrum Pin
9062	Bobbin Case Retainer Fulcrum Pin Set Screw
9063	Bobbin Case Retainer Fulcrum Pin Spring
9074	Bobbin Case Retainer Latch
9068-B	Bobbin Case Retainer Adjusting Screw
9073	Bobbin Case Retainer Latch Pin
9066	Bobbin Case Retainer Latch Spring
9067-AB	Bobbin Case Retainer, (Assem.)
9070	Belt (Rubber)
9080-A	Face Plate (Assem.)
9081-B	Face Plate Thread Guide
104-C	Face Plate Thread Guide Rivet
9006	Face Plate Screw (2 used)
9083	Feed Shaft
9087	Feed and Feed Lift Eccentric
9088	Feed Eccentric Screw
9089	Feed Eccentric Lever
9090	Feed Eccentric Lever Fulcrum Screw
9103-B	Feed Bar
9092	Feed Bar Spring
9093	Feed Bar Fulcrum Stud
9028	Feed Bar Fulcrum Stud Set Screw
9094-B	Feed Bar Operating Lever
9095-B	Feed Bar Operating Lever Fulcrum Screw
9096-B	Feed Point
9101-B	Feed Point Screw (2 used)
9098	Feed Shaft Gear
9017	Feed Shaft Gear Set Screw (2 used)
C-400	Gauge
9205	Gauge Screw

PARTS LIST

No. Part	Name
9110	Hook
4836	Hook Set Screw
9112-A	Hook Cover (Assem.)
9115	Hook Shaft
9116	Hook Shaft Bushing (Front)
9117	Hook Shaft Bushing (Rear)
9086	Hook Shaft Bushing Set Screw (2 used)
9118	Hook Shaft Spur Gear
9017	Hook Shaft Spur Gear Screw (2 used)
9119	Hook Shaft Bevel Gear
9017	Hook Shaft Bevel Gear Screw (2 used)
9125-A	Lamp Shade and Socket (Assem.)
9126	Lamp Shade Bracket
9127	Lamp Shade Bracket Screw
9128	Lamp Shade Socket Clamp Screw
9129-B	Motor Screws (2 used)
B9129-B	Motor Screw Washer (2 used)
9432	Motor Cover Plate
9433	Motor Cover Plate Screw (4 used)
9434	Motor Pulley
9435	Motor Pulley Set Screw
9130-B	Needle Bar
9131	Needle Bar Cap
9133	Needle Bar Crank
9134	Needle Bar Crank Set Screw
9135	Needle Bar and Take-up Crank
9136	Needle Bar and Take-up Crank Pin
9137-A	Needle Bar Crank and Take-up Crank, (Assem.)
9138	Needle Bar Link
9139	Needle Bar Yoke
9019	Needle Bar Yoke Screw
9140-B	Needle Clamp
311-C	Needle Clamp Screw
9141	Needle Plate
9142	Needle Plate Screw (2 used)
9179	Oil Tube

PARTS LIST

Part No.	Name
9150	Presser Bar
9151	Presser Bar Spring
B316D	Presser Bar Spring Adjusting Cap
9152	Presser Bar Guide
9153	Presser Bar Guide Screw
9154	Presser Bar Lifter
9155	Presser Bar Lifter Screw
323-C	Presser Foot
325	Presser Foot Nut
324-F	Presser Foot Thumb Nut
9165-A	Stitch Regulating Lever (Assem.)
9166	Stitch Regulating Lever Fulcrum Screw
9168	Stitch Indicating Plate
9169	Stitch Indicating Plate Rivet (4 used)
9180	Take-up Crank
9181	Take-up Lever
9182	Take-up Lever Screw
9183	Take-up Yoke Rod
9184	Take-up Yoke Rod Set Screw
9185-A	Take-up, (Assem.)
9186	Take-up Yoke
9187	Take-up Fulcrum Stud
9019	Take-up Fulcrum Stud Set Screw
9188	Tension Stud
9189	Tension Stud Set Screw
9190	Tension Nut
9191	Tension Spring
F.O.129	Tension Disc (2 used)
9193	Tension Release Plate
9194	Tension Release Pin
9195	Tension Release Lever
9196	Tension Release Lever Fulcrum Stud
9028	Tension Release Lever Fulcrum Stud Set Screw
9198	Tension Spring Take-up
9201	Thread Cutter
9199	Thread Guide (Upper)
9200	Thread Guide (Lower)

MECHANICAL OPERATION

The *Sewhandy* mechanical operation follows the normal sewing machine mechanical arrangement used in the 1920's.

It has a low rear motor providing power thru a rubber belt to the Belt Wheel. The Belt Wheel is mechanically connected to the Hook Shaft. Note that the Belt or Hand Wheel is mounted low on the *Sewhandy*. Compare this to the SINGER Featherweight Model 221 where it is high on the machine.

Theoretically, having the rotating mass of the Belt Wheel low on the machine creates a low center-of-gravity. This produces a more stable machine with less motor torque/speed change reaction and vibration.

In contrast, the newer (1933) design of the SINGER Featherweight Model 221 has the spinning mass of the Hand Wheel about 3.5 inches higher than the *Sewhandy*. Because of this the SINGER 221 has a much higher center-of-gravity and a lower stability factor.

The *Sewhandy* mechanical operation is broken down into three separate functional areas: 1) Shafts and Gears, 2) Needle Drive, and 3) Feed and Hook Drive.

Shafts and Gears

In operation, the motor and Belt Wheel rotate in a clockwise direction as viewed from the right side or front. Since the main drive shaft (Hook Shaft) is connected to the Belt Wheel, it also rotates in the clockwise direction. See the drawing below.

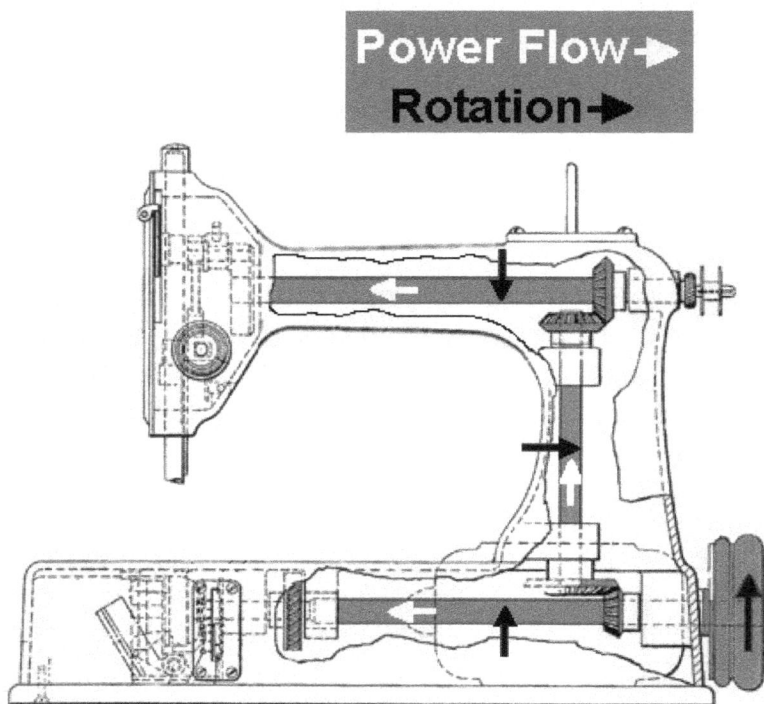

The 3/8th inch diameter Hook Shaft connects to the 5/16th inch diameter Arm Shaft (Vertical) thru a brass bevel gear set. The Arm Shaft (Vertical) rotates in a counter clockwise direction. It connects thru a brass miter gear set to the 5/16th inch diameter Arm Shaft (Top) that also rotates in counter clockwise direction (as viewed from the Belt Wheel end).

There are bushings and bushing supports for each drive shaft. Each bushing has its own oil hole to provide for lubrication replenishment. Oil hole location is identified in the Preventative Maintenance chapter. Bushing locations are shown in the drawing below.

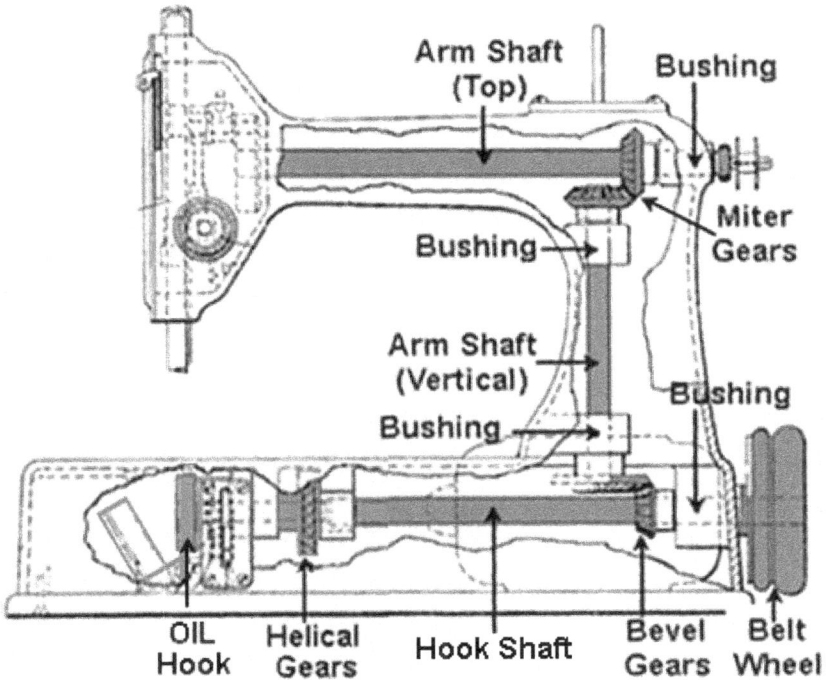

The bevel gears on the Hook Shaft and Arm Shaft (Vertical) are straight cut gears with a gear ratio of 1:2 (18 teeth and 36 teeth). The Arm Shaft (Top) and Arm Shaft (Vertical) Miter

Gears are a special type of straight cut bevel gear designed to operate in pairs with identical numbers of teeth (24) and diametrical pitch, and a 1:1 gear ratio. Brass gears are used because the constant meshing work hardens the teeth allowing them to last longer.

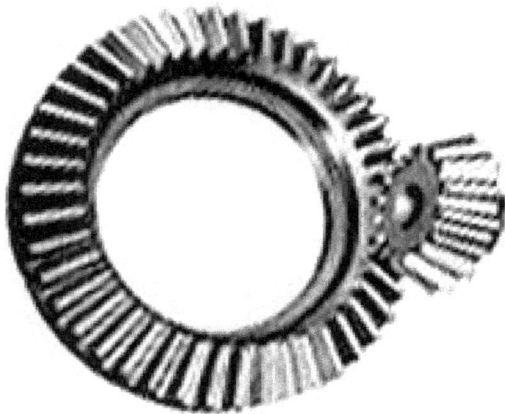

Bevel Gears

Miter Gears

Needle Drive

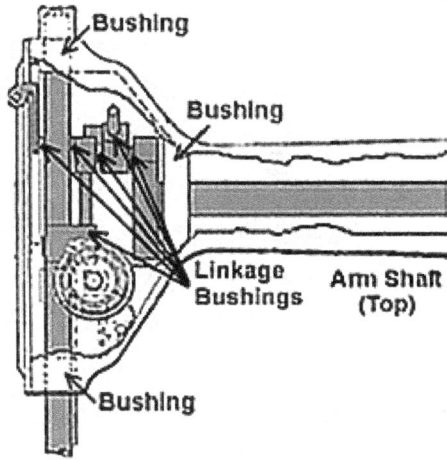

The counter clockwise rotating Arm Shaft (Top) provides power thru the bushing support to the Needle Bar and Take-up Crank. This connects and provides power to both the Needle Drive and the Take-up Lever.

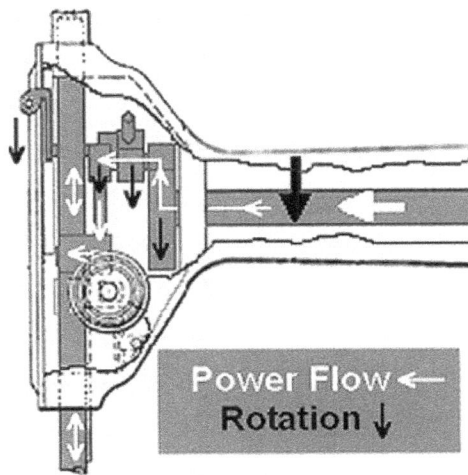

The Needle Drive power flow is shown below. The power flow is from the Needle Bar and Take-up Crank (larger right white arrow) thru the Take-up Yoke (larger left white arrow) thru the Needle Bar Yoke (thinner white arrow) thru the Needle Bar link thru the Needle Bar Clamp thru the Needle Bar (double headed white arrow) to the Needle. This process changes the Arm Shaft (Top) rotational movement into the up-down movement of the needle. It also maintains the exact timing relative to the Feed Shaft and Hook Drive.

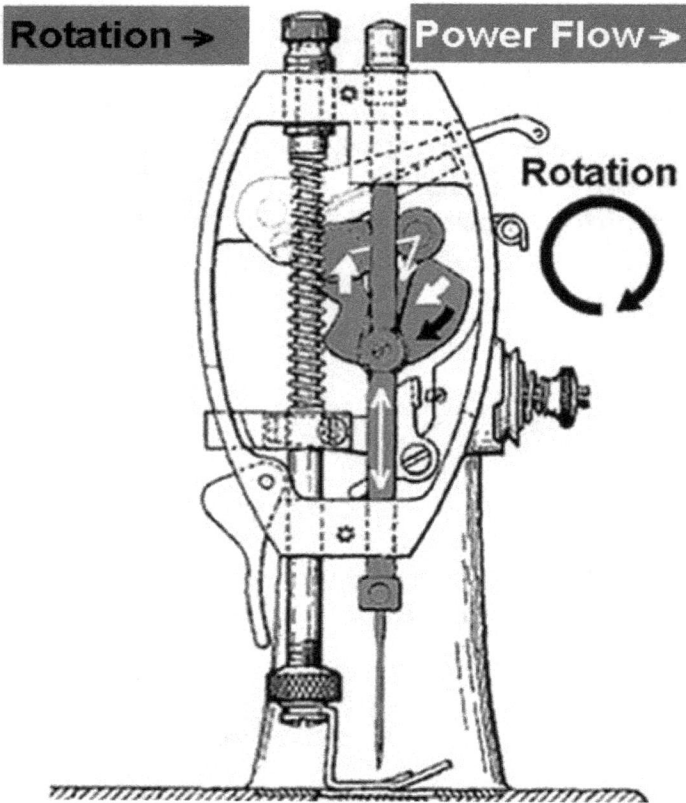

The Take-up Lever power flow is shown below. The power flow is from the Needle Bar and Take-up Crank (right white arrow) thru the Take-up Yoke (center white arrow) thru the Take-up Yoke Rod thru the Take-up Crank (left white arrow) thru the Take-up Fulcrum to the Take-up Lever. This process changes the Arm Shaft (Top) rotational movement into the up-down movement of the Take-up Lever. It also maintains the exact timing relative to the Feed Shaft and Hook Drive.

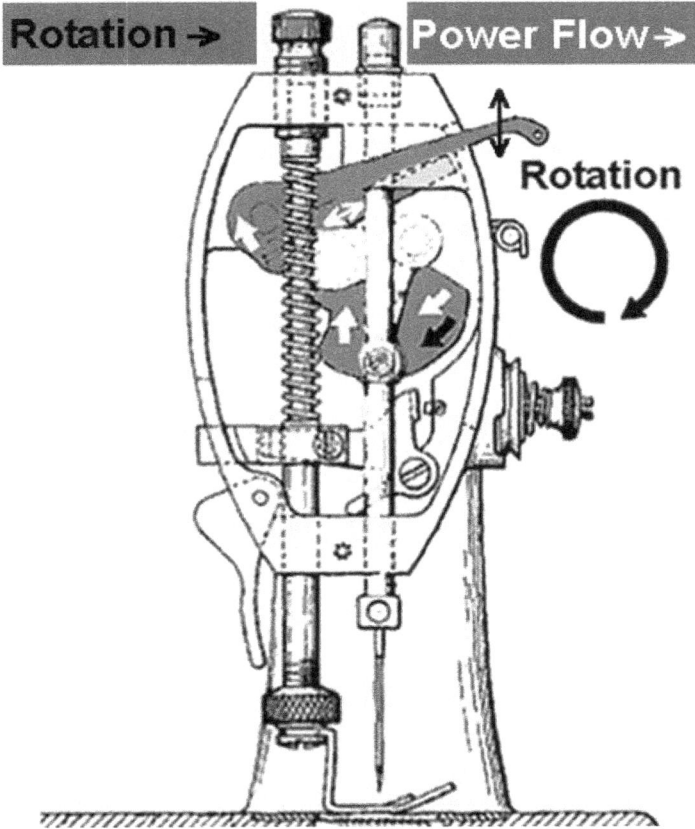

Feed and Hook Drive

The Feed and Hook Drive is powered by the rotating Hook Shaft. The power flow is shown below. The Feed power flow is from the Hook Shaft spur gear thru the Feed Shaft gear. The Hook Shaft spur gear is a brass helical left-hand gear with 15 teeth, while the Feed Shaft gear is a brass helical right-hand gear with 30 teeth (ratio is 1:2).

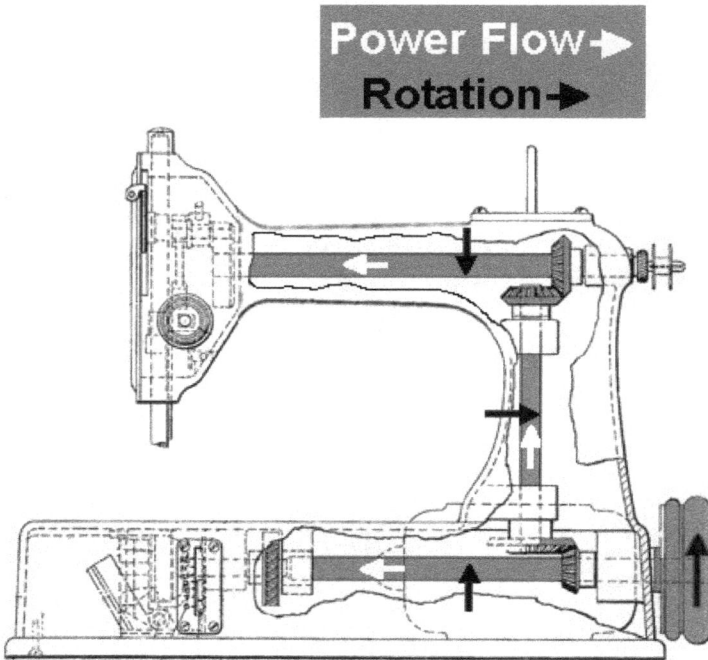

Power Flow→
Rotation→

The Feed Shaft gear is mounted on one end of the Feed Shaft. The shaft rides on the center bushing support. The other end of the shaft is machined with two different shaped cam lobes.

These lobes create the forward and back, and up and down movement of the Feed Dogs.

Left-Hand
Helical Gear

Right-Hand
Helical Gear

Left-Hand Gear teeth lean to the left
when the gear is placed flat on a
horizontal surface. Right-Hand Gear
teeth lean to the right when the gear
is placed flat on a horizontal surface.

Left-Hand (top) and
Right-Hand (bottom)
Helical Gears
meshing.

89

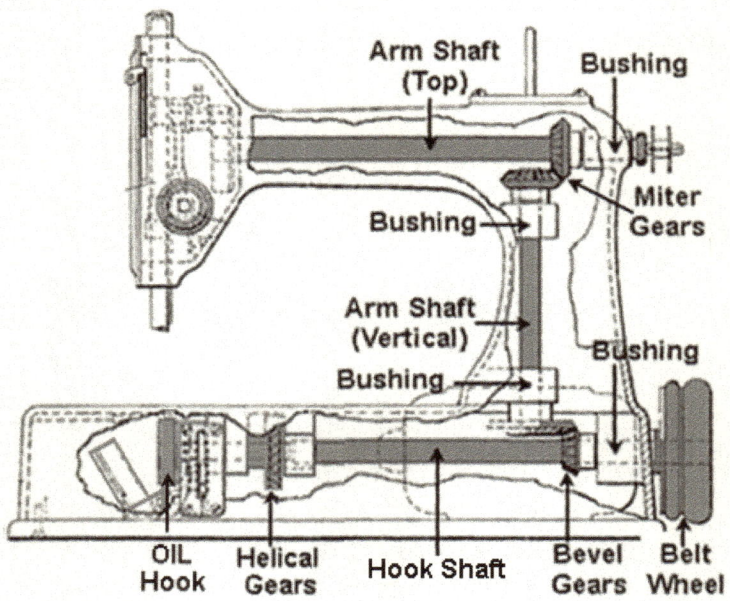

Arm Shaft (Top) · Bushing · Miter Gears · Bushing · Arm Shaft (Vertical) · Bushing · Bushing

OIL Hook · Helical Gears · Hook Shaft · Bevel Gears · Belt Wheel

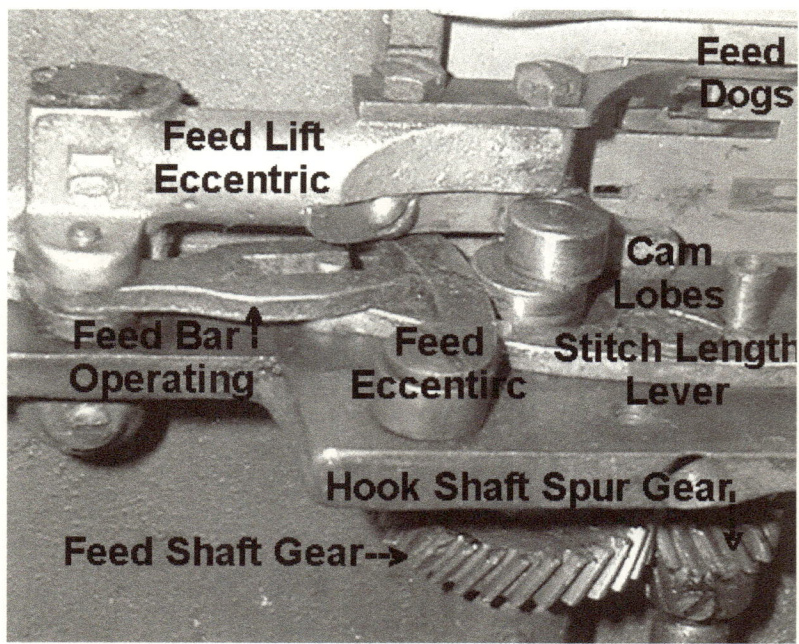

Feed Dogs · Feed Lift Eccentric · Cam Lobes · Feed Bar Operating · Feed Eccentirc · Stitch Length Lever · Hook Shaft Spur Gear · Feed Shaft Gear-->

The forward and backward movement of the Feed Dogs is produced by the Feed Eccentric riding on the clockwise rotating cam lobe. The movement flow proceeds from the Feed Eccentric thru the Feed Bar Operating Lever thru the Feed Lift Eccentric to the Feed Dogs. The black arrows in the photo below show the movement path.

The up and down movement of the Feed Dogs is produced by the Feed Lift Eccentric riding on the clockwise rotating end cam lobe. The movement flow proceeds from the Feed Lift Eccentric to the

Feed Dogs. The black arrows in the photo below show the movement path.

You can also see the **Stitch Length Lever** that rides in a slot in the **Feed Bar Operating lever** in the photos.

At the bottom right corner bottom of the photos are shown the two helical brass gears, the **Feed Shaft gear** (left and rotating clockwise from this end) and the **Hook Shaft Spur gear** (right and rotating counter clockwise from this end).

The Hook Drive power flow is directly from the Hook Shaft. The shaft rides on another center bushing support. The Hook/Shuttle is mounted with two setscrews on the end of the Hook Shaft.

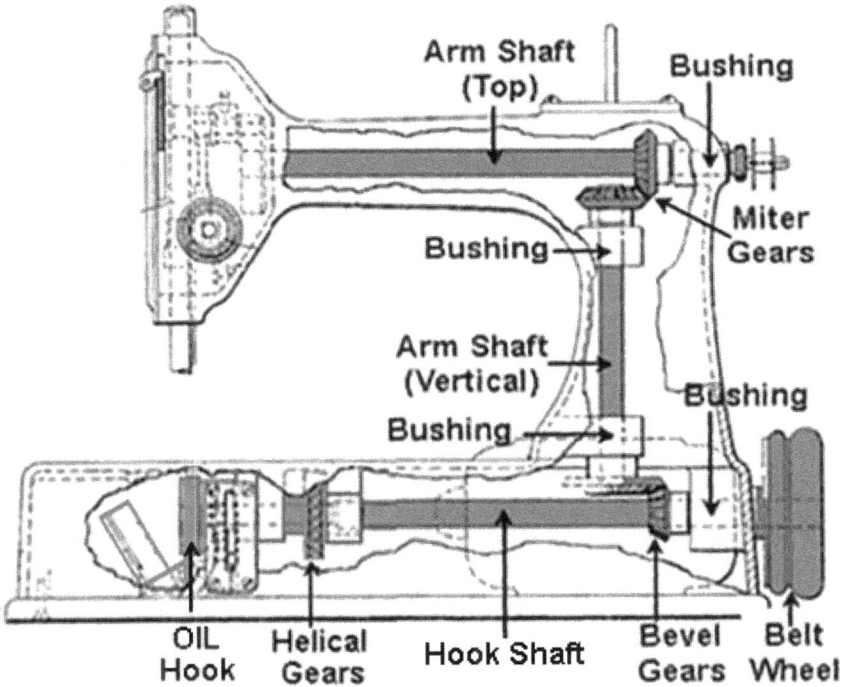

The Bobbin Case and Bobbin ride inside the Hook. Keeping both Bobbin Case and Bobbin in their correct position inside the Hook is the Bobbin Case Retainer.

As with most sewing machines, the rotation of the Hook (shuttle) timed with the downward then upward needle stroke catches the thread loop and forms the chain-stitch.

ELECTRICAL OPERATION

The *Sewhandy* has a fairly simple electrical circuit. Note that the system, as manufactured, does not use a polarized or grounded 3-prong plug. There is always a risk of shock when using these older electrical systems. (The *Sewhandy* can be rewired to use the 3-prong grounded system. Contact author by email for price). The electrical system consists of the following:

- Black Cloth covered two-conductor Main Power cord from the 120VAC wall outlet (male 2-prong plug) to the power input connector (female 2prong plug).
- Rear input power connector (male 2 prong plug).
- Foot Pedal with two-conductor power cord connecting with front of machine (male 2-prong plug).
- Front Foot Pedal power connector (female 2-prong plug).
- Black Cloth covered single conductor wire from Rear input power connector to Drive Motor.
- Black Cloth covered single conductor wire from Rear input power connector to Front Foot Pedal power connector (female 2-prong plug).
- Black cloth covered two-conductor cord from Rear input power connector Lamp assembly.

- **Black Cloth covered single conductor wire from Front Foot Pedal power connector (female 2-prong plug) to Drive Motor.**
- **Lamp Assembly with side rotary switch.**
- **Sewing Machine Drive Motor**

Theory of Operation

Plug the Foot Pedal power cord 2–prong male connector into the front 2-prong female connector. Plug the machine female 2-prong connector on the Main Power cord into the male 2-prong connector on the rear of the machine. Plug the Main Power cord 2-prong male connector into a 120VAC power source, i.e. switched power strip. The *Sewhandy* is now ready to operate. It does not have a main power on-off switch.

You can test for power to the *Sewhandy* by turning the Lamp Assembly switch on. The light will now be lit. Pressing on the Foot Pedal will cause the Drive Motor to rotate.

How does all this work? The 120VAC *HOT* side current at the power strip moves thru the Main Power Cord to the Rear Input power connector. Here it connects with the *Hot* (Black) wire going to the Front Foot Pedal power connector. It also connects thru a two-conductor cord to the Lamp Assembly rotary switch. The *Hot* continues thru the Front Foot Pedal power cord to the Foot Pedal. The Foot Pedal has a Resistive Element that limits the current and the motor speed. The now variable current leaves the Foot Pedal out thru the Foot Pedal Power cord to the other contact of the 2-prong Front Foot Pedal power connector. The variable current continues thru the wire to the Drive Motor. The variable current is felt across the brushes and windings and causes the Drive Motor to spin if there is an electrical return or neutral path.

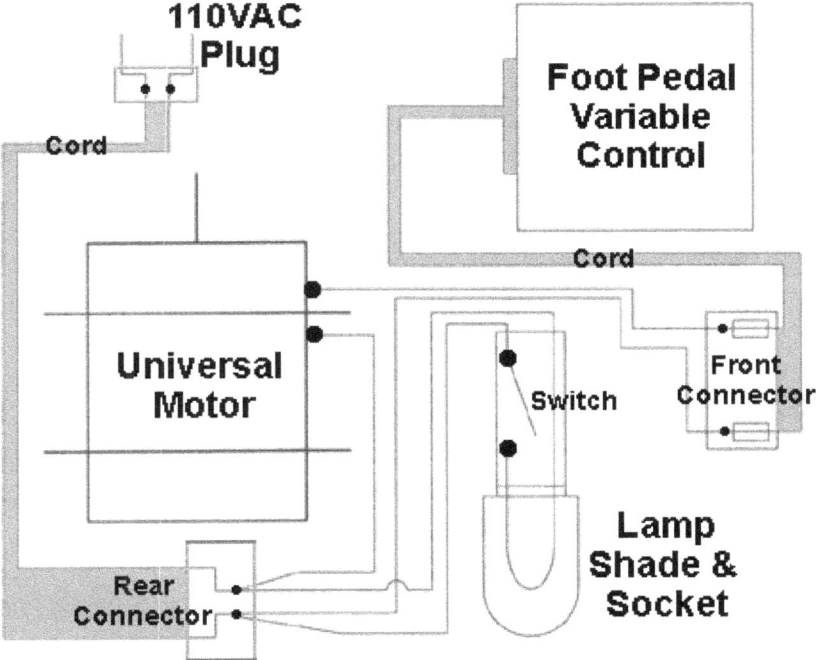

The neutral path continues out of the Drive Motor thru the wire to the Rear Input power connector. The return path continues thru the Main Power cord to the 120VAC power strip neutral.

The Lamp Assembly circuit is powered from the *Hot* side of the Rear Input power connector as explained previously. The return or neutral for the Lamp Assembly is thru the other conductor of the two-conductor cord to the neutral side of the Rear Input power connector. As before, the return path continues thru the Main Power cord to the 120VAC power strip neutral.

Motor Theory & Breakdown

There are two different motors used on the *Sewhandy* and GE *MODEL A*. The GE motor is used on all models except for the OSANN SINGER *Sewhandy*. The OSANN SINGER *Sewhandy* uses a SINGER BRK/BUK series motor. Both motors are Universal type motors.

Universal Motors

GE and SINGER used the Universal or Commutator motor in the *Sewhandy* because the universal motor operates at much higher speeds than an induction motor and delivers more power than a similar size induction motor.

The universal motor is a single-phase commutated motor with wound field coils in series with a DC type armature (wound rotor). Universal motors can be powered by either DC or AC. The have a rotor or armature with coils of wire wound around it. They also have a rotating cylinder or commutator with alternating strips of conducting and nonconducting material.

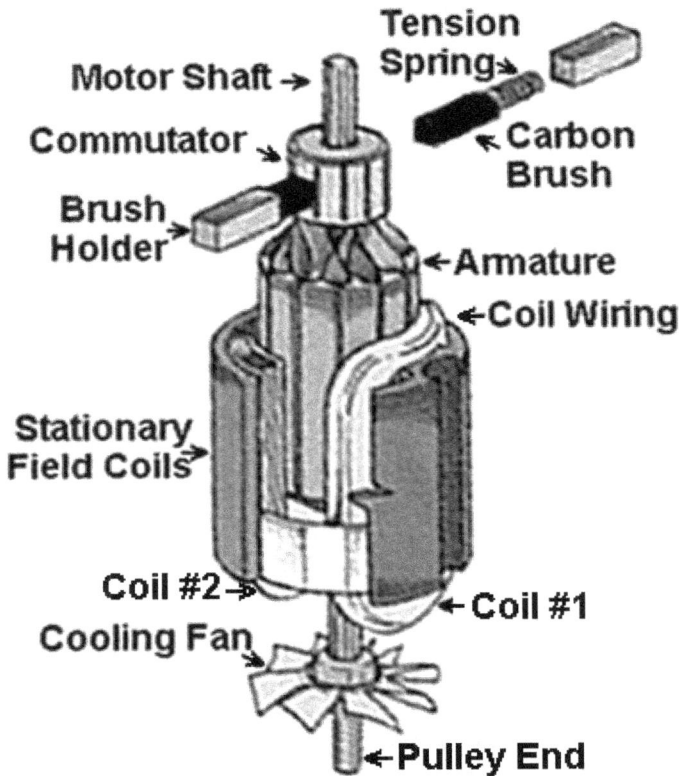

Tension Spring→

Motor Shaft →

Commutator →

←Carbon Brush

Brush Holder→

←Armature

←Coil Wiring

Stationary Field Coils→

Coil #2→

←Coil #1

Cooling Fan→

←Pulley End

The armature and the commutator are mounted on the motor shaft. A carbon brush on each side of the commutator transfers current from the electrical circuit. These brushes are soft blocks of carbon with a spring attached to provide slight pressure and compensate for wear. When the carbon brushes slip over the commutator surface, the armature is magnetized and rotates. This provides the rotation that powers the sewing machine. Most universal motors also have a cooling fan at the end of the shaft.

The most frequent failure of universal motors is the carbon brushes wearing down. When they wear down, the motor will spark and electrical contact will become intermittent. Carbon brushes are replaceable. See the section on Motor Disassembly for more information.

GE Motor

The GE motor is a typical Universal Electrical sewing machine unit. On the drive end there is a belt pulley mounted to the shaft.

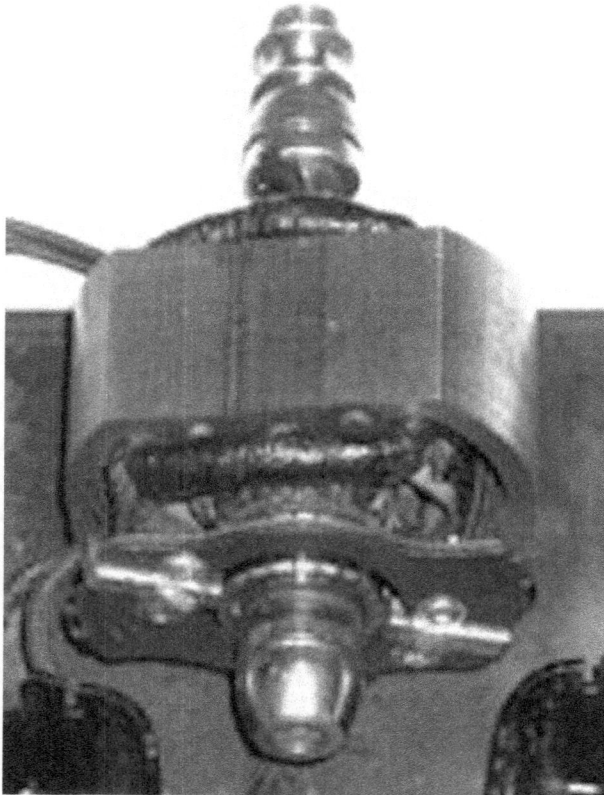

The bushing support assembly is the same on both ends, and is made of steel with a bronze bushing insert. This is what the shaft spins on. Both bushing support assemblies are grooved to fit onto the motor housings.

Farther down the drive shaft are 4 fiber spacer washers, and a 3 bladed fan. Next is the 2-3/4th inch long by 1-3/8th inch diameter commutator and winding brush assembly. The non-drive end bushing support assembly is last on the shaft.

The two brush assemblies are of the carbon with spring design. See the chapter on Replacing Consumables on page 235 for the size of the carbon brushes.

The brushes are held in the Brush Holder assembly. The assembly has two brass brush holders mounted 180 degrees apart on a fiberboard. Wires connect the brass brush holders to the Winding assembly. Motor disassembly and Brush replacement are not difficult. However, see the following chapter on Preventative Maintenance for more instructions and hints before starting.

SINGER BRK/BUK Motor

The **SINGER BRK/BUK** motor is also a typical Universal Electrical sewing machine unit. The BRK/BUK series motor is illustrated below. Note that the **SINGER BRK/BUK** motors installed in the *Sewhandy* do not have the outer sheet metal and **SINGER** metal label installed.

SINGER BUK Motor

On the drive end there is a belt pulley mounted to the shaft. The bushing support assembly is cast in the housing, and is the same on both ends, and is made of steel with a bronze bushing insert. This is what the shaft spins on.

The two brush assemblies are of the carbon with spring design. See the chapter on Replacing Consumables for the size of the carbon brushes.

The brushes are held in the Brush Holder assembly. The assembly has two brass brush holders mounted 180 degrees apart on a fiberboard. Wires connect the brass brush holders to the Winding assembly.

Motor disassembly and Brush replacement are not difficult. However, see the following chapter on Preventative Maintenance for more instructions and hints before starting.

Form K3691

This Book should be carefully preserved for reference

INSTRUCTIONS

FOR USING AND ADJUSTING

SINGER

B.U.K. ELECTRIC MOTORS

WITH FOOT CONTROLLER FOR
FAMILY SEWING MACHINES

When requiring
Needles, Oil,
Parts or Repairs
for your Machine

Look for the
Red "S"
There are Singer
Shops in every City

THE SINGER MANUFACTURING CO.

1931

All Rights Reserved

Foot Pedal Theory and breakdown

The original Foot Pedal supplied with all *Sewhandy* models is made by General Electric. There are two 110VAC models, and they are both black metal unit as pictured below. (Note that other universal foot pedals may be used.)

The GE Pedals are stamped with General Electric and the Pat # 1,728,004 (filed March 31, 1926 and granted September 10, 1929). The older model with a circular Resistive Element is GE Cat # 2068556GR, while the newer model with a rectangular Resistive Element is GE Cat #4294783GR 2. The inventor of this design was

Marvin L. Norris of Fort Wayne, Indiana. Note: There is also a 220VAC export Foot Pedal model with the GE Cat # #4294783GR 3. It also erroneously marked with the US Pat # 1,72<u>6</u>,004 instead of the correct 1,72<u>8</u>,004. The export model will not work with any <u>110VAC</u> *Sewhandy*.

The Foot Pedal electrical theory follows: The two-conductor electrical cord provides 110VAC from the *Sewhandy* Front Connector. The *Hot* side goes directly to Terminal 20. This terminal also connects with the Resistive Element block. Also connected to the Resistive Element block are Terminals 15 –19.

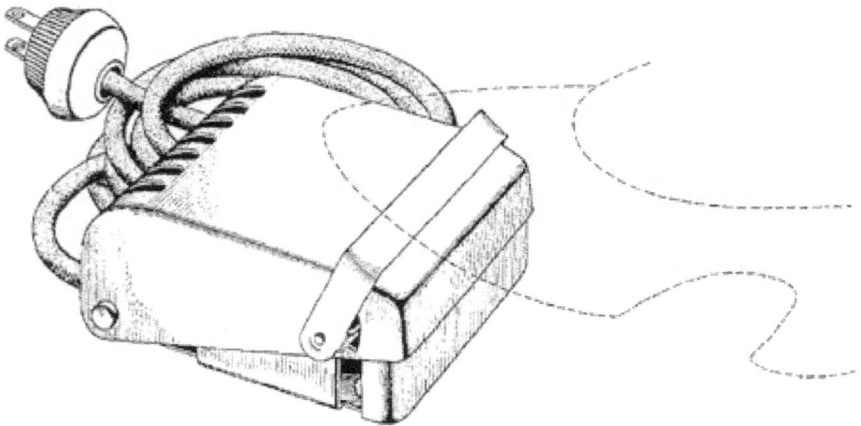

The Resistive Element block is designed so that Terminal 20 has no resistance to the circuit *Hot* side. However, Terminal 19 will have some resistance, Terminal 18 will have more than 19, Terminal 17 will have more than 18, Terminal 16

will have more than 17, and Terminal 15 will have more than any of the others.

Each of the terminals connects to a normally open pressure switch. In the actual design, these switches are individual conductive fingers connected to a bridging assembly. When the finger contacts the *Hot* Terminal(15–20), the Hot side flows across that switch to the Bridging Bus or Assembly thru Terminal 33 and out the cord to the other plug contact. This provides a variable *Hot* to the *Sewhandy* thru the front connector. Refer to the Theory of Operation on the previous pages for where it goes next.

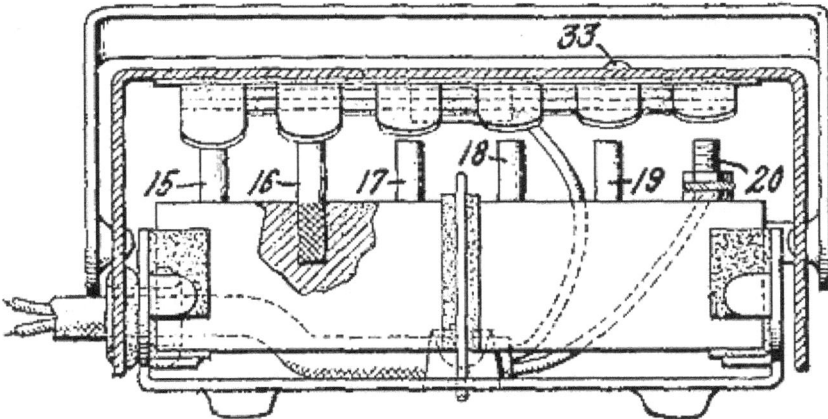

The Foot Pedal design is such that with no pressure on it, there are no fingers or switches contacting, and no electrical flow.

With slight pressure, finger 15 connects and a minimum current is allowed across to the

Bridging Bus. Remember, Terminal 15 has the maximum resistance and will only allow a low amount of current or amperage to pass.

With slightly more pressure, finger 16 connects (along with 15) and additional current is allowed across to the Bridging Bus. Remember, Terminal 16 has the slightly less resistance than 15 and will allow a greater amount of current or amperage to pass.

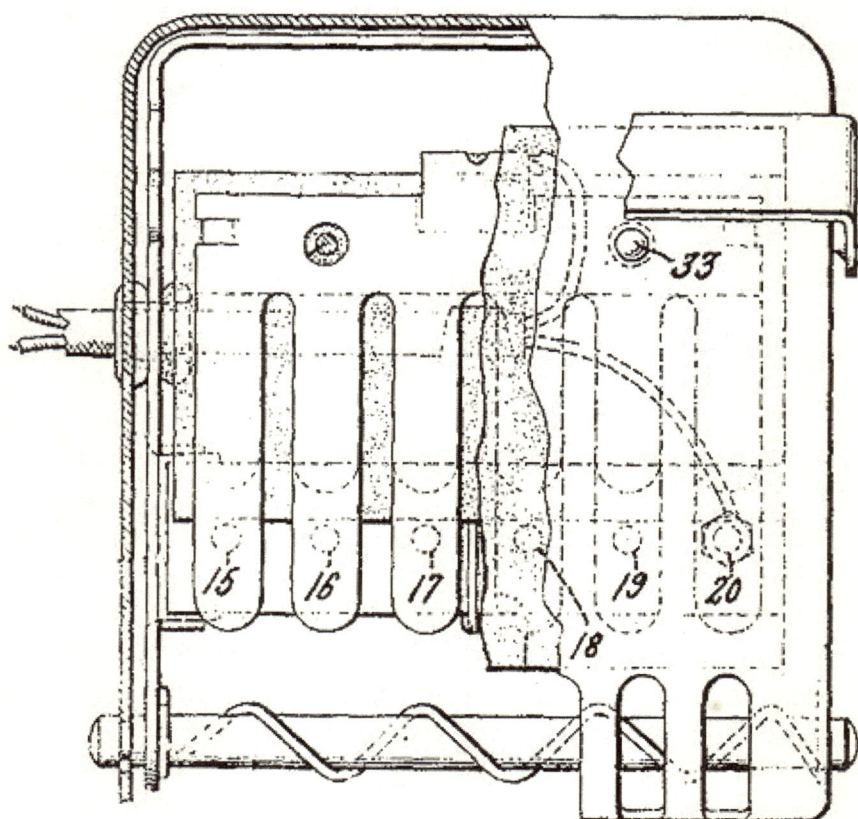

With even more pressure, finger 17 connects (along with 15 and 16) and additional current is allowed across to the Bridging Bus. Remember, Terminal 17 has the slightly less resistance than 16 and will allow a greater amount of current or amperage to pass.

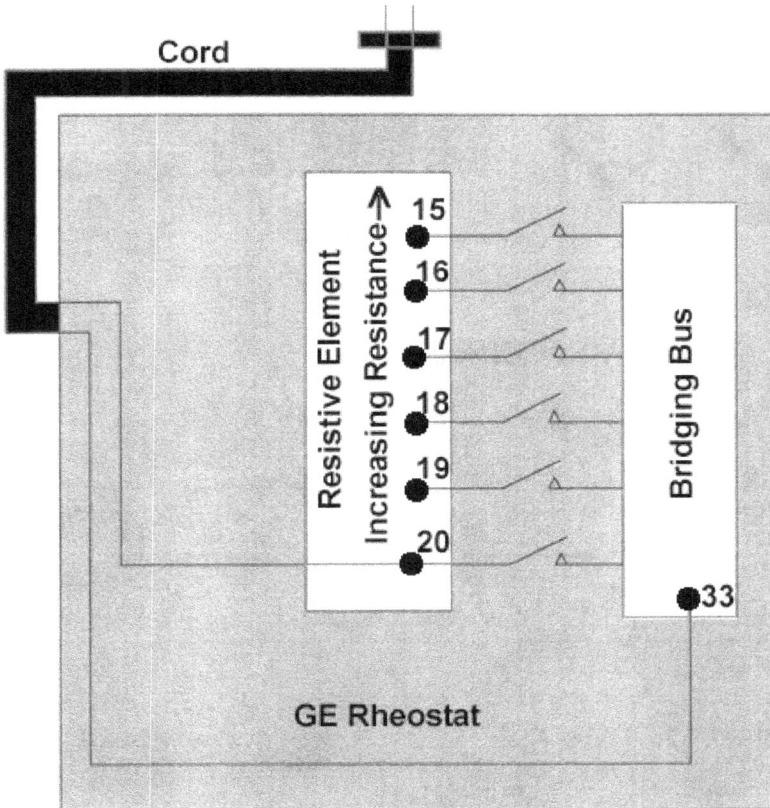

With more pressure, finger 18 connects (along with 15, 16, and 17) and additional current is allowed across to the Bridging Bus. Remember, Terminal 18 has the slightly less resistance than

17 and will allow a greater amount of current or amperage to pass.

With still more pressure, finger 19 connects (along with 15, 16, 17, and 18) and additional current is allowed across to the Bridging Bus. Remember, Terminal 19 has the slightly less resistance than 18 and will allow a greater amount of current or amperage to pass.

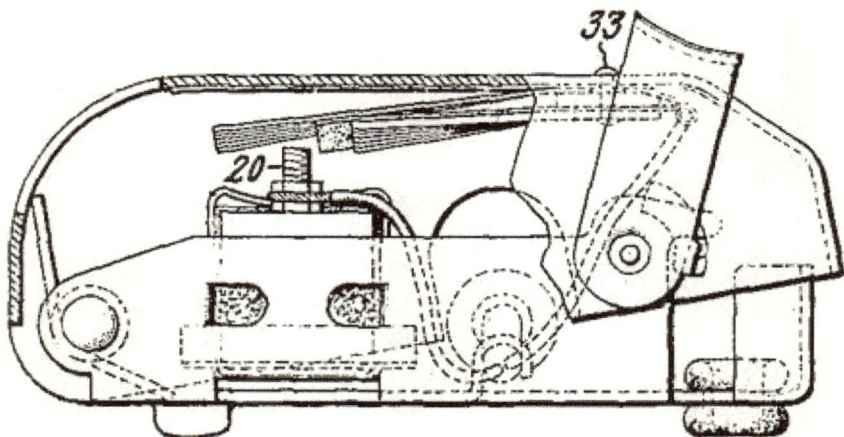

In addition to each Terminal 15 thru 19 finger or switch individually allowing more current or amperage to pass, they also have an additive effect (as parallel resistors) on the total current or amperage passed. Simply, if Terminal 15 conducts 0.05 amps by itself, and Terminal 16 conducts 0.10 amps by itself, then the two of them together would conduct 0.15 amps.

With maximum pressure, finger 20 connects and allows the maximum current required by the motor across to the Bridging Bus. Remember, Terminal 20 has no resistance between it and the *Hot* side. The parallel resistor arrangement has no effect on the output of Terminal 20 because it is already allowing the maximum current that the motor requires.

It is very important to remember that this is a non-polarized and an ungrounded system. The design of the interior of the Foot Pedal is such that the outer case is insulated from the *Hot* side. It must remain insulated at all times.

Also, take note that neither wire nor circuit side in the Foot Pedal is the neutral.... **Both sides are Hot.** One side has the maximum available (i.e. wall outlet 15 amps or power strip 3 amps), while the other is variable with maximum to no amperage.

For your safety, I strongly recommend using a low amperage power strip with your *Sewhandy* or Featherweight. Also, discontinue Foot Pedal use immediately if you notice smoke or heat, or smell something odd.

While I have presented the Foot Pedal theory here, I do not recommend that you disassemble it or try to repair it. An error in reassembly could cause the ungrounded outer case to become part of the 120VAC *Hot* circuit with disastrous results for the Foot Pedal, and painful results for you. Let a professional sewing machine technician take the risks on this one.

PREVENTATIVE MAINTENANCE

Preventative maintenance is defined as maintenance performed while a machine is still in working order to keep it from eventually breaking down. This includes the tasks of lubricating, tightening, and replacing worn parts

Completely read and understand all instructions and hints before beginning a task. If you are not comfortable performing any adjustment or maintenance on the *Sewhandy*, take it to your sewing machine technician, or send it to me.

Maintenance Tune-ups

Regular maintenance tune-ups or adjustments are a necessary part of extending the life of your sewing machine. Your *Sewhandy* is now over 70 years old, and with care will last for another 70 years.

The manufacturers recommend that all sewing machines, even modern ones, have a maintenance tune-up every one to two years. Under daily usage, the time drops to every six months. Whether you have your sewing machine technician perform it or whether you do it makes no difference as long as all the steps are performed correctly. (Note: The following information is not a recommendation that you perform this maintenance. You are the only one that knows whether you are capable

113

o f performing the preventative maintenance or not.

1. If you haven't already done so, remove the belt from the motor pulley and the belt wheel.
2. Unscrew the two screws holding on the Lamp Shade and Socket Assembly. Gently lay it aside. (It will still be hooked to the electrical cable). See picture below.

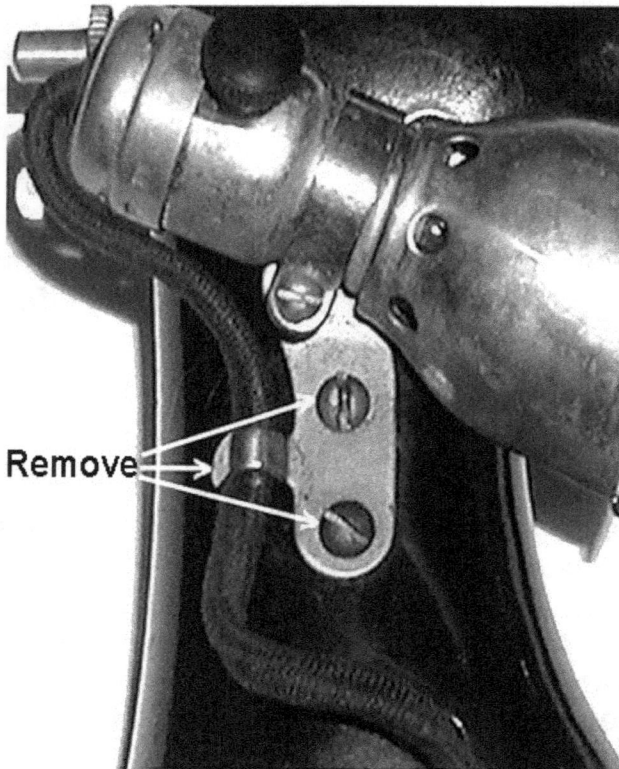

Remove

3. Remove two screws holding the Spool Pin and Plate. Remove Spool Pin and Plate.

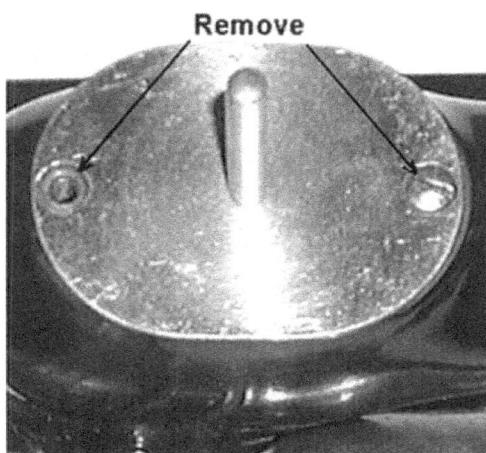
Remove

4. **Insert small piece of cloth or towel into the access hole to keep anything else from getting to the gears.**

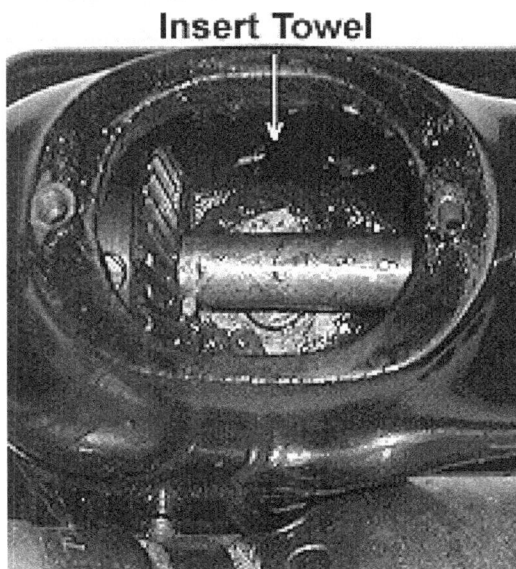
Insert Towel

5. **Gently turn the *Sewhandy* over so that you are looking at the wooden bottom.**

6. <u>Only remove the **FIVE** screws</u> that I have indicated in the picture below. Removal of the other screws will make everything much more difficult.

Only Remove These 5 Screws

7. While holding the neck of the *Sewhandy* in one hand and supporting the wooden base with the other hand, slowly lift the two assemblies apart.
8. Let the non-motor end of the wooden base tilt farther down. This will let the motor pulley slide though the hole in the bed.
9. Carefully guide the Lamp Shade and Socket Assembly with its cable thru the motor hole.
10. You now have two separate parts: The sewing machine bed Mechanical assembly, and the Bottom Electrical assembly. Set the Bottom Electrical assembly safely aside.

11. Remove as many of the covers as practical: the Slide Plate, Needle plate, Face Plate, and Top Arm Cover. The goal is to expose as much of the inside of the *Sewhandy* as possible. I suggest that you use a magnetic holder to keep all the screws together in one place.
12. Use a small brush and some type of pick or tweezers to remove visible thread and lint. Make sure that you get in to all the nooks and crannies, i.e. between the feed dogs, under and around the hook, and in the shuttle raceway. Make sure you turn the machine bed over and inspect it from the bottom.
13. Use a vacuum cleaner to suck out any additional thread and lint. DO NOT USE COMPRESSED AIR, CANNED AIR, OR A VACUUM TO BLOW AIR INTO THE *SEWHANDY*!! While many recommend blowing trash out of the machine, there is too much of a risk of blowing stuff farther into the machine (along with blowing it all over the room).
14. Check for old thread wound around the take-up lever and links, under the hook and bobbin case, the feed dogs and levers, and around the tension assembly, belt wheel, and motor pulley.
15. Check for burrs or scratches on the hook (shuttle). If you can catch your fingernail on a scratch, then it has to be repaired. Either of these defects will catch the thread and delay

loop formation. Blend with rubber sanding strip as necessary.

16. Check for loose screws and connections. However, do not over tighten the screws as the threads will strip. Use the correct size screwdriver for this so that you do not damage the screw slot.

17. Check for gears not properly meshing and for broken gear teeth. Gently use a dental pick to get in between gear teeth and pick out any accumulated grease or lint. Check for gear endplay by gently attempting to move gear side to side. There should be minimal movement, if any. Remember to look and note whether the gears are dry or have lubrication, i.e. grease is visible.

18. Give the *Sewhandy* machine bed section one more complete look-over.

19. Move on to the bottom electrical section.

Use a small brush and some type of pick or tweezers to remove visible thread and lint. Make sure that you get in to all the areas between the wires and plugs, and under and around the motor. (Not: Do not disturb the two asbestos spacer pads under the motor).

20. Use a vacuum cleaner to suck out any additional thread and lint. **DO NOT USE COMPRESSED AIR, CANNED AIR, OR A VACUUM TO BLOW AIR INTO THE *SEWHANDY*!!**

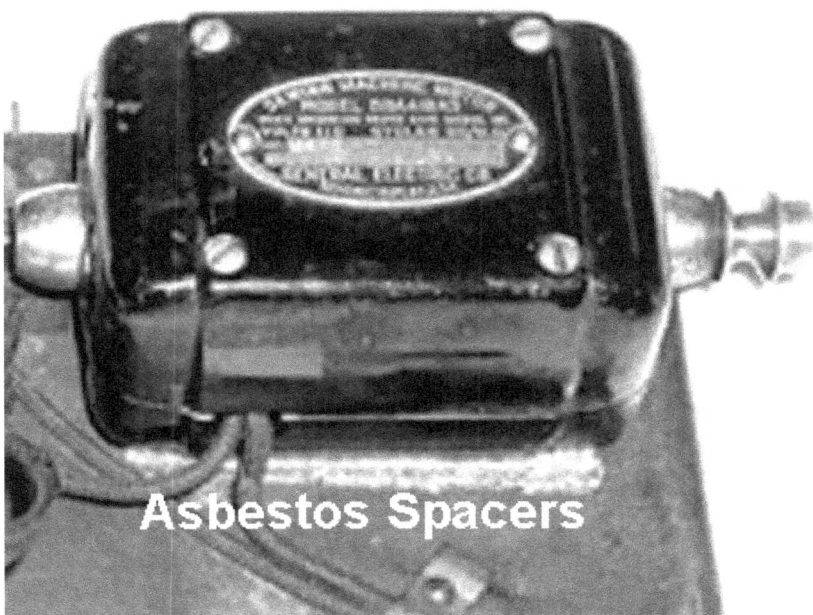

Asbestos Spacers

21. **DO NOT BLOW AIR AT THE TWO ASBESTOS SPACER PADS UNDER THE MOTOR!** While many recommend blowing trash out of the machine, there is too much of a risk of blowing stuff farther into the machine (along with blowing it all over the room).
22. Check all the wiring for deterioration and damage. Remember that the *Sewhandy* has a

non-grounded electrical system with no protection other than the 70-year-old wire insulation between you and the 120VAC Hot wire. If you find <u>ANY DAMAGE</u>, have it repaired or replaced before operating your *Sewhandy*. Email me for assistance.

23. Check the motor for noise by rotating it clockwise by hand. Check the motor for end play by grasping the motor pulley and gently pulling-pushing on it. There should be minimal movement. Read more about the motor on pages 98 and 137.

24. Lubricate the machine. Refer to the Chapter on Lubrication on page 127.

25. Give everything one final check before starting to put the bottom electrical section and the machine bed section back together.

26. Carefully guide the Lamp Shade and Socket Assembly with its cable thru the top motor hole of the *Sewhandy* machine bed section.

27. Let the non-motor end of the wooden base tilt farther down. This will let the motor pulley slide into the machine pulley hole.

28. Carefully fit the two assemblies together. Pay close attention to the front and rear electrical connectors. They need to fit into their openings without damaging them. Remember that the connectors are old and brittle.

29. Once everything fits together evenly, install the five screws that you originally removed. It is easier if you start with the center screw and then move to the corner screws.

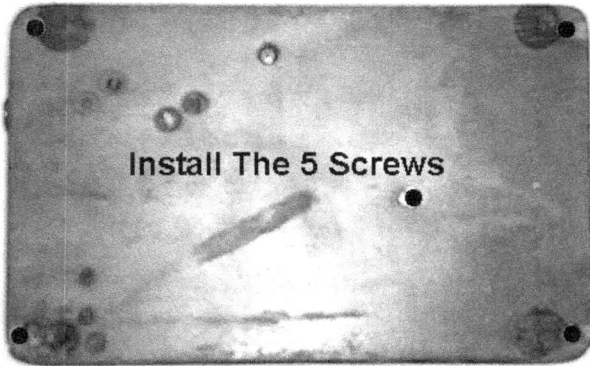

Install The 5 Screws

30. Do not tighten the screws, but check Bottom and Machine Assemblies for proper fit.
31. If satisfied, snug screws down, but do not over tighten.
32. Turn machine correct side up, and reinstall Lamp Shade and Socket Assembly with the two screws previously removed.

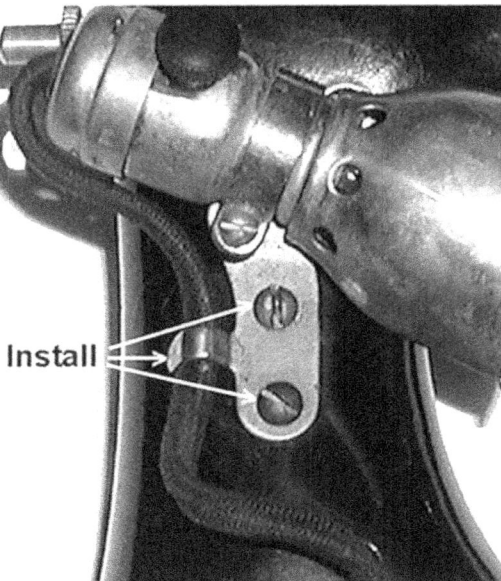

Install

33. Remove any cloth or towel from Spool Pin access hole. Check that nothing has gotten into the gears, and insure that gears are lubricated with white lithium grease.

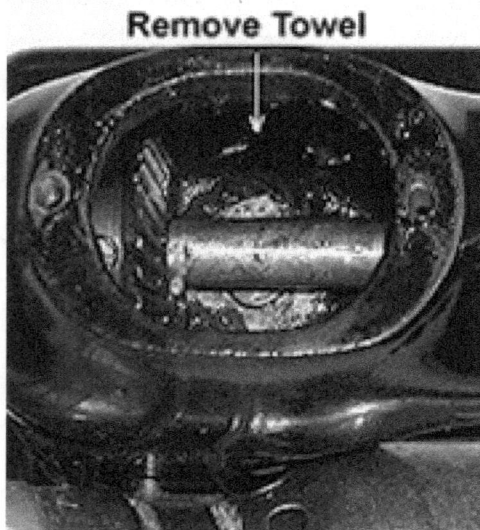

Remove Towel

34. Reinstall the screws, Spool Pin, and Plate.

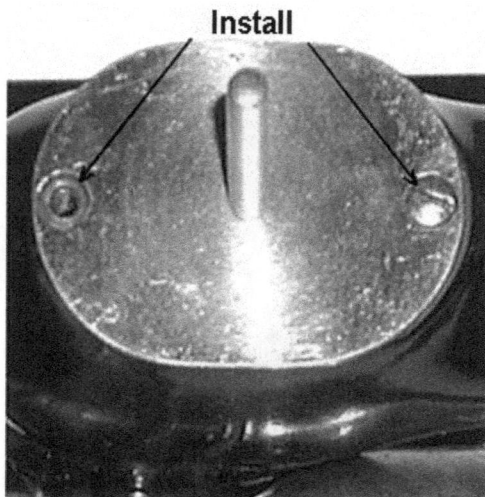

Install

35. Reinstall drive belt. Check for the correct tension. It should be tight enough to prevent slipping, but not so tight that it causes the machine to slow down. If it is too tight it will drastically shorten the life of the motor.
36. Replace the covers. Remove any burrs or damage from the Needle Plate and replace it and the Slide Plate if necessary.
37. Disassemble the Tension Assembly, and clean between the disks. Make sure that you remove all corrosion. The discs must be smooth for consistent top thread tension. Use emery cloth as needed to smooth out the surface of the discs. Reassemble the Tension Assembly when finished. Ensure that the check spring is functioning properly.
38. Clean the Bobbin Case and Bobbin case spring. Reassemble the Bobbin case when finished.
39. Make preliminary tension adjustments. See the Chapter on Tension on page 217. Adjust the bobbin case tension by the "drop" method or by using a calibrated spring scale. Example shown below.

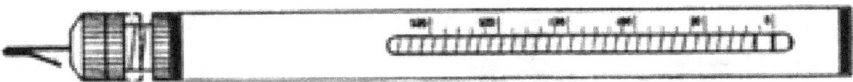

40. Adjust the needle top tension assembly. See the Chapter on Tension on page 217. Adjust the top tension using "trial and error" or by using a calibrated spring scale. Example shown above.

41. Insert a new needle, and thread the machine.
42. Check for any dripping oil. Remove excess oil as necessary.
43. Inspect Foot pedal and wiring for any deterioration and damage. Remember that the *Sewhandy* has a non-grounded electrical system with no protection other than the 70-year-old wire insulation between you and the 120VAC Hot wire. If you find **ANY DAMAGE**, have it repaired or replaced before operating your *Sewhandy*. Email me for assistance.
44. Plug Foot pedal power cord into front 2-prong female connector.
45. Plug Main Power cord into rear input 2-prong mail connector.
46. Plug Main Power cord into 120VAC power.
47. <u>Slowly</u> press down on Foot pedal and power the drive motor.
48. Run motor slowly for a few minutes.
49. Watch for and listen for anything unusual, i.e. smoke, noise, etc. Immediately disconnect power if you suspect a problem. If there is a problem I recommend that you take it to your Sewing Machine Technician or email me.
50. Sew a sample, and evaluate the top and bottom stitch formation. Make final tension adjustments to the needle top tension assembly and the bobbin case spring. See the Chapter on Tension on page 217.
51. Use a mild detergent to clean the outside of the *Sewhandy* gently, but thoroughly.
52. To protect the exterior paint finish and the decals, treat it like an expensive classic car.

I recommend using a premium carnauba auto wax. Use only the wax type, not the combination cleaner/wax. One coat rubbed in coat will protect the exterior. Note: Keep the wax out of the mechanical parts, i.e. tensioner, levers, shafts, pulleys, and belt.

53. After the *Sewhandy* has completely cooled down, put it back in its case. Do not put a <u>warm machine in the case</u> as it will build up moisture and begin to corrode.

LUBRICATION

By definition, Lubrication should be part of the Preventative Maintenance section. However, proper Lubrication is so important to the operation and life of a sewing machine that I have made it a separate chapter.

When we speak of sewing machine lubrication, we usually mean two types: oil and grease.

Sewing machine oil <u>is not</u> the motor oil that you use for your car. Automotive oil is completely different and is never acceptable for use in any sewing machine. Sewing machine oil is clear white synthetic or mineral light oil with a low viscosity (i.e. 4.0). Be sure to use the proper oil.

Do not ever oil the tension discs or the belt on any machine. These items require friction to operate correctly and oiling them will minimize the required friction. If you do get oil on them, a <u>little</u> alcohol on a wipe will usually clean the oil off. Note: Excess alcohol will damage the rubber belt just like any petroleum product.

The trick about oiling your *Sewhandy* is not to use too much oil. One or two drops should be sufficient in each oil hole. Run the machine by hand to distribute the oil into all the bearings. Note that if your *Sewhandy* leaves an oil puddle on the table each time you use it, you are using way too much oil.

All antique and vintage sewing machines have many oil holes. If they did not have all those oil holes, then they would already be worn out and junked. Luckily for us, the *Sewhandy* has an oil hole for each bearing (bushing) surface. The next few pages identify the location and the bushing lubricated by each oil hole.

In addition to the designated oil holes, the *Sewhandy* manual recommends"take the bobbin case out and *put a drop or two on the bobbin case bearing surface* of the hook...each time you start...two or three times" in an 8 hour period.

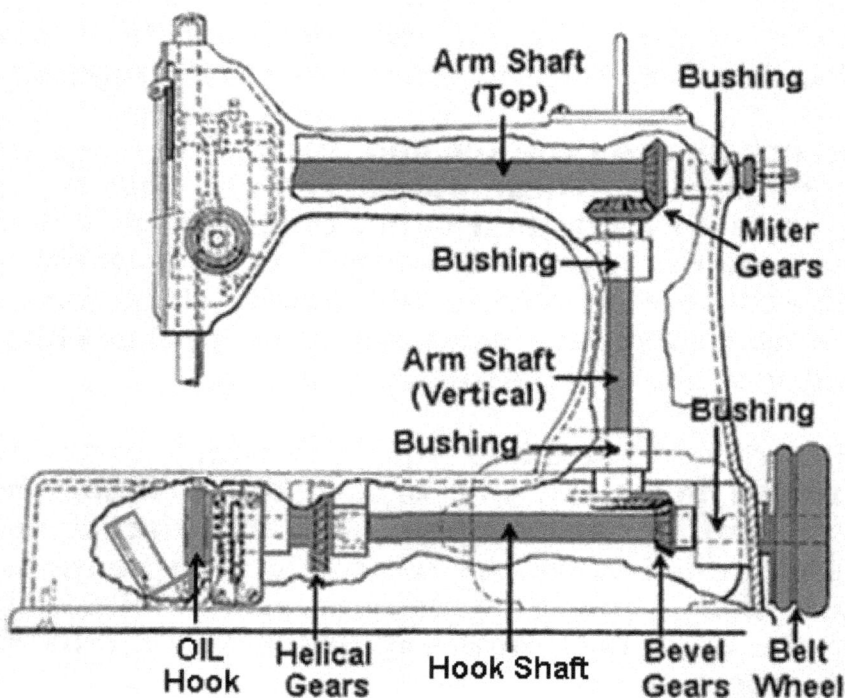

Arm Shaft (Top) — Bushing — Miter Gears — Bushing — Arm Shaft (Vertical) — Bushing — Bushing — OIL Hook — Helical Gears — Hook Shaft — Bevel Gears — Belt Wheel

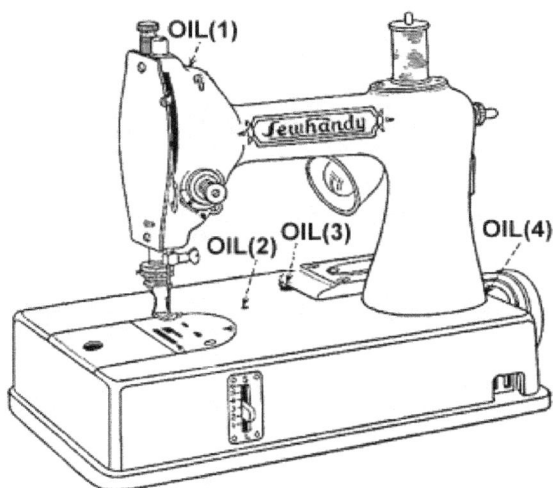

OIL(1)

Sewhandy

OIL(2) OIL(3) OIL(4)

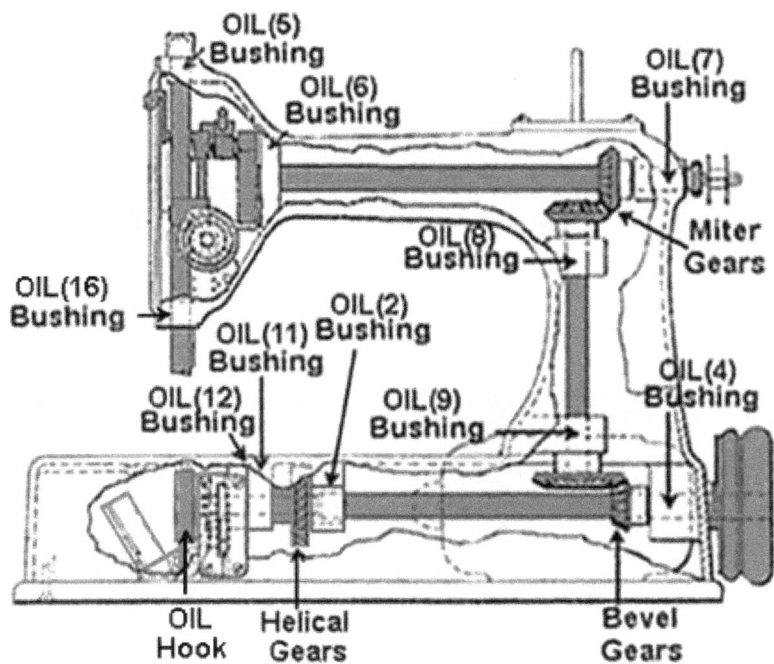

OIL(5)
Bushing
OIL(6)
Bushing
OIL(7)
Bushing

OIL(8)
Bushing
Miter
Gears

OIL(16)
Bushing
OIL(2)
Bushing
OIL(11)
Bushing
OIL(4)
Bushing
OIL(12)
Bushing
OIL(9)
Bushing

OIL
Hook
Helical
Gears
Bevel
Gears

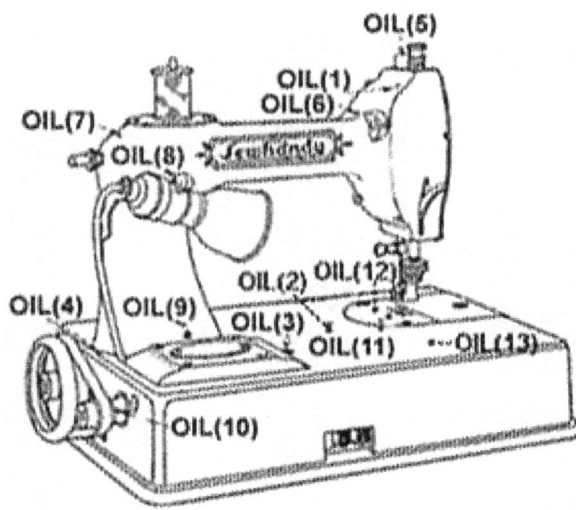

OIL(5)

OIL(1)
OIL(6)

OIL(7)

OIL(8)

OIL(2) OIL(12)

OIL(4)   OIL(9)

OIL(3)

OIL(11)   OIL(13)

OIL(10)

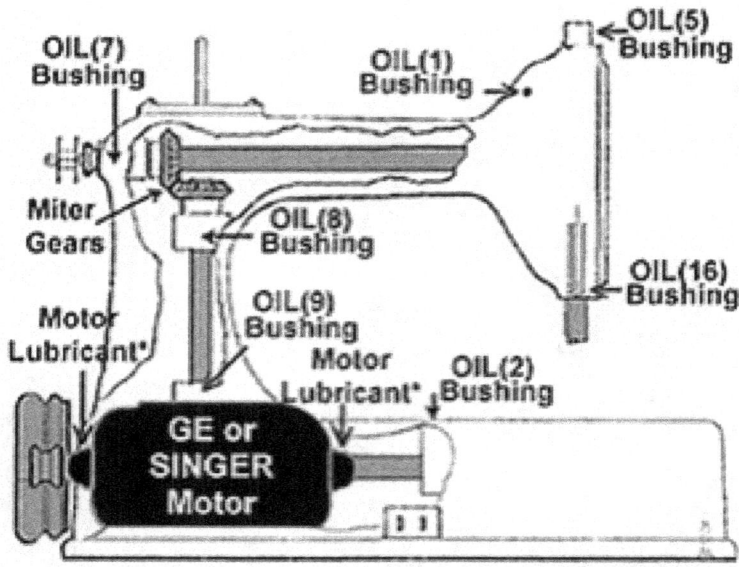

OIL(7)
Bushing

OIL(1)
Bushing

OIL(5)
Bushing

Miter
Gears

OIL(8)
Bushing

OIL(16)
Bushing

Motor
Lubricant*

OIL(9)
Bushing

Motor
Lubricant*

OIL(2)
Bushing

GE or
SINGER
Motor

*- GE Motor uses Sewing Machine Oil
*- SINGER OSANN Motor uses SINGER
Sewing Machine Lubricant
Bevel/Miter Gears use White Lithium Grease

130

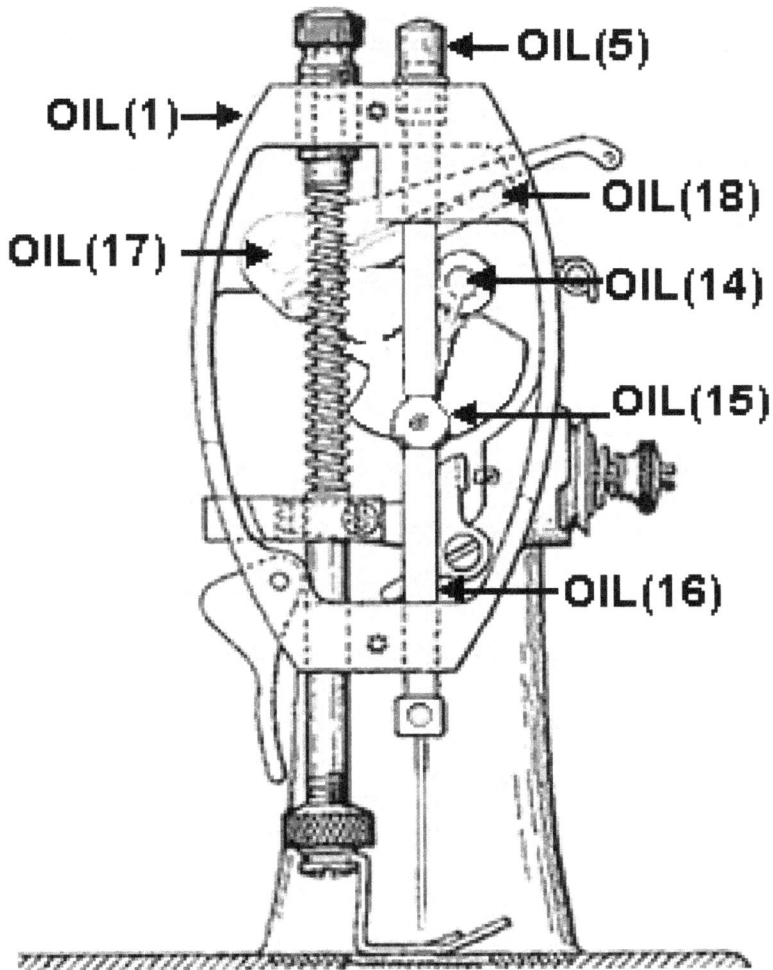

OIL(1)→

OIL(5)

OIL(18)

OIL(17)

OIL(14)

OIL(15)

OIL(16)

Oil Hole 1: Take-up Yoke
Oil Hole 2: Feed Shaft Right Bushing
Oil Hole 3: Motor Bushing (GE Motor Only)
Oil Hole 4: Hook Shaft/Belt Wheel Bushing
Oil Hole 5: Needle Bar Top Bushing
Oil Hole 6: Arm Shaft (Top) Left Bushing
Oil Hole 7: Arm Shaft (Top) Right Bushing

Oil Hole 8: Arm Shaft (Vertical) Top Bushing
Oil Hole 9: Arm Shaft (Vertical) Bottom Bushing
Oil Hole 10: Motor Bushing (GE Motor Only)
Oil Hole 11: Feed Shaft Left Bushing
Oil Hole 12: Hook Shaft Left Bushing
Oil Hole 13: Feed Bar Stud Bushing
Oil Hole 14: Needle Bar Yoke
Oil Hole 15: Needle Bar Link
Oil Hole 16: Needle Bar Lower Bushing
Oil Hole 17: Take-up Lever Bushing
Oil Hole 18: Take-up Yoke Rod Bushing

The original *Sewhandy* manual advises "frequently" oiling the machine. While this will not hurt the *Sewhandy*, it is a waste of good sewing machine oil and creates a mess. A more reasonable schedule would be after 8 hours of actual sewing place one drop of oil in each oil hole. Also occasionally oil any metal surface contacting or rubbing against another. After oiling and lubricating your *Sewhandy*, wipe away excess oil. Run stitches on some fabric scraps before you tackle your sewing project.

Like all other petroleum products, common sense and safety rules do apply. Watch out for oil splashing into your eyes. Do not rub your eyes while your hands are oily. Refer to the product warning or MSDS info for safety information.

The GE Motor also requires regular oiling, but the SINGER-OSANN Motor requires regular SINGER Lubricant- NOT OIL.

GE Motor – Oil Only

SINGER Motor – SINGER Lubricant only

The three brass gear sets (Miter, Bevel, and Helical) should <u>never be oiled</u>. The problem with oiling the gears is that oil is a dust magnet, and causes the dust to adhere to the brass gears wearing down the teeth.

The *Sewhandy* manual recommends using Vaseline to lubricate the gears. Today, a better choice is white lithium grease. White lithium grease has lithium compounds that give the grease a better performance and temperature range. It also adheres well to metal and resists flying off the gears from centrifugal force. With white lithium grease, you should only have to re-grease the *Sewhandy* gears every three or four years.

If you put oil where grease is supposed to be, any grease that was there will usually soften and just run out. What is left is a little oil, and a soon-to-be dry part.

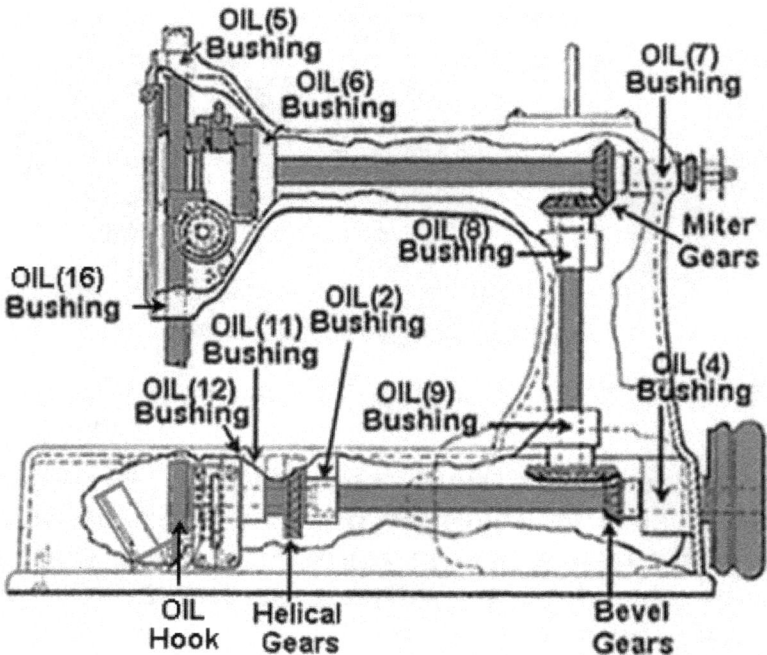

MITER GEARS

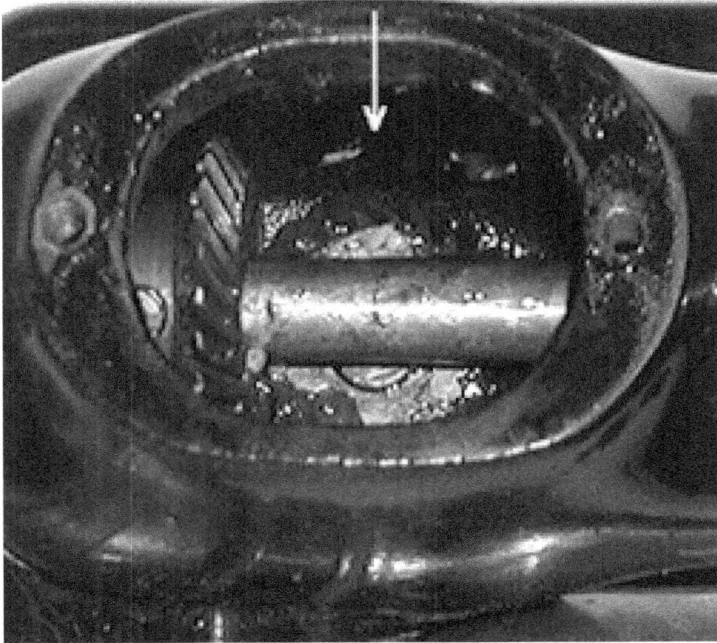

BEVEL GEARS

HELICAL GEARS

Remember, with white lithium grease you should only have to re-grease the *Sewhandy* gears every three or four years.

Foot Pedal Lubrication

I do not recommend any lubrication of the Foot Pedal. All oil is flammable and Foot Pedals do get hot. Additionally, any excess oil will attack and accelerate deterioration of the electrical wire insulation. Refer any Foot Pedal lubrication to your sewing machine technician. If you do not have one, I can provide maintenance support.

MOTOR DISASSEMBLY & BRUSH REPLACEMENT

This section details the breakdown of the two types of drive motors, and the replacement of the two carbon brush and spring assemblies. The GE Motor is described first; the OSANN SINGER Motor is second.

Note: If you do not feel confident in performing these tasks, do not attempt them. You may damage the motor parts and replacement will be difficult.

These instructions are not a recommendation that you perform them, but are here as educational information. (Email me for service prices or see www.SewingMachineTech.com).

GE Motor Disassembly & Brush Replacement

Disassembly steps:

1. Remove ALL POWER from *Sewhandy*.
2. Disconnect all electrical cords.
3. Remove the Drive belt.
4. Unscrew the two screws holding on the Lamp Shade and Socket Assembly. Gently lay it aside. (It will still be hooked to the electrical cable). See picture on next page.

Remove

5. Remove two screws holding Spool Pin and Plate. Remove Spool Pin and Plate.

Remove

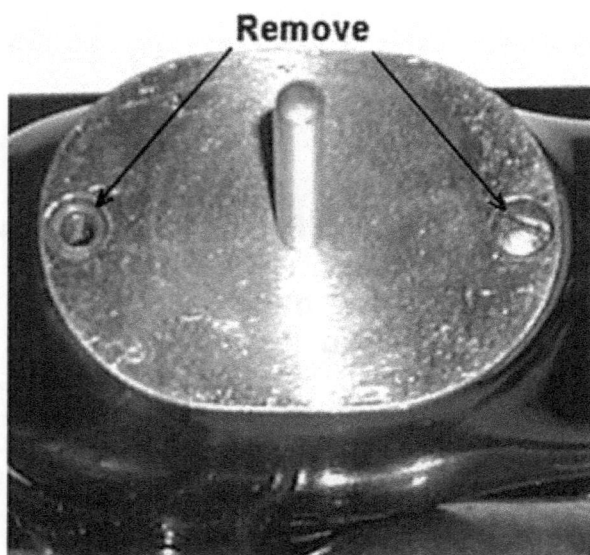

6. Insert small piece of cloth or towel into the access hole to keep anything else from getting to the gears.

Insert Towel

7. Gently turn the *Sewhandy* over so that you are looking at the wooden bottom.
8. <u>Only remove the FIVE screws</u> that I have indicated in following the picture. Removal of the other screws will make everything much more difficult.

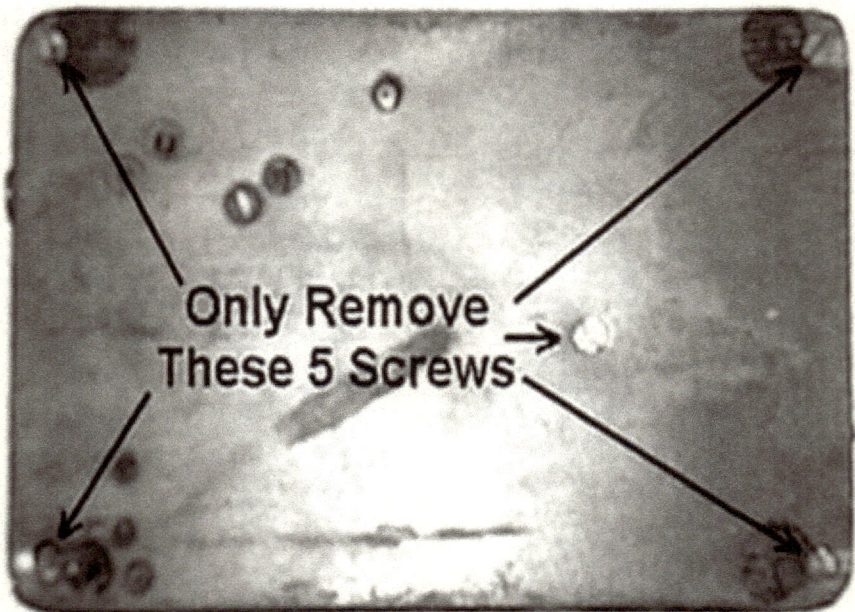

Only Remove
These 5 Screws

9. While holding the neck of the *Sewhandy* in one hand and supporting the wooden base with the other hand, slowly lift the two assemblies apart.
10. Let the non-motor end of the wooden base tilt farther down. This will let the motor pulley slide though the machine hole.
11. Carefully guide the Lamp Shade and Socket Assembly with its cable thru the top motor hole.
12. You now have two separate parts: The sewing machine Mechanical assembly, and the Bottom Electrical assembly. Set the Mechanical assembly safely aside.

13. Note that there are two **ASBESTOS** spacer pads underneath the bottom of the motor. **DO NOT DISTURB** them.

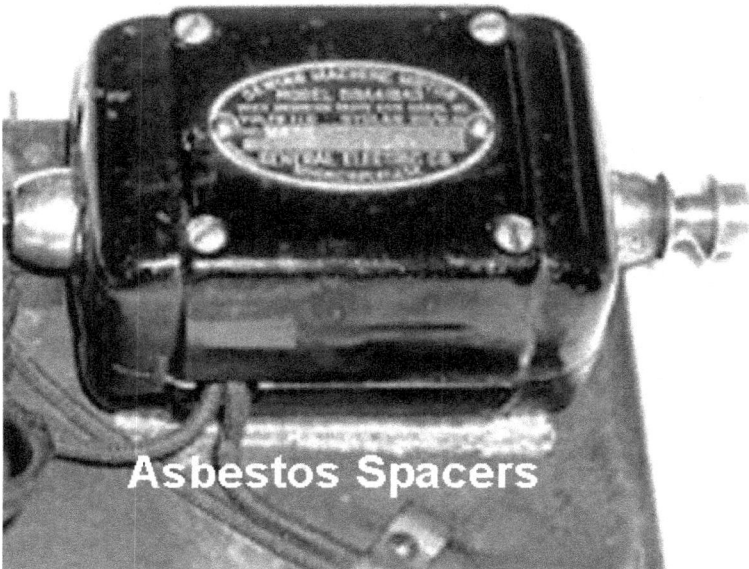

Asbestos Spacers

14. **Remove the four screws on the motor top housing assembly.**

15. **Gently pull upward on the top motor housing assembly.**
16. **Note that everything may come with the top housing assembly or it may stay with the bottom housing assembly.**
17. **Using soft pliers, grab the steel bushing support assembly on the pulley end, and rotate it slightly. This will move it out of the housing assembly hole. Repeat on the other bushing support assembly. The Commutator will now be free of the housing assembly. <u>STOP! Do not remove it yet</u>.**
18. **The Brush Holder assembly fits in grooves in the top and bottom housing assemblies. Gently pry with an awl or small screwdriver to free it from the housing assembly.**

Brush Holder Assembly Grooves

19. You cannot remove the Carbon Brush and Spring Assemblies until after you remove the commutator assembly. <u>Do not destroy the top of the Brass Brush holders by attempting to remove them that way</u>!

20. Remove the commutator assembly by from the pulley end.

21. The carbon brush and spring assemblies can now be removed for replacement. <u>Only take one carbon Brush and Spring assembly out at a time, and note the exact position of the carbon brush in its holder</u>. This will allow you to correctly reinstall the carbon brush if necessary. Pay special attention to the position of the concave end in relation to the commutator segments contact surface.

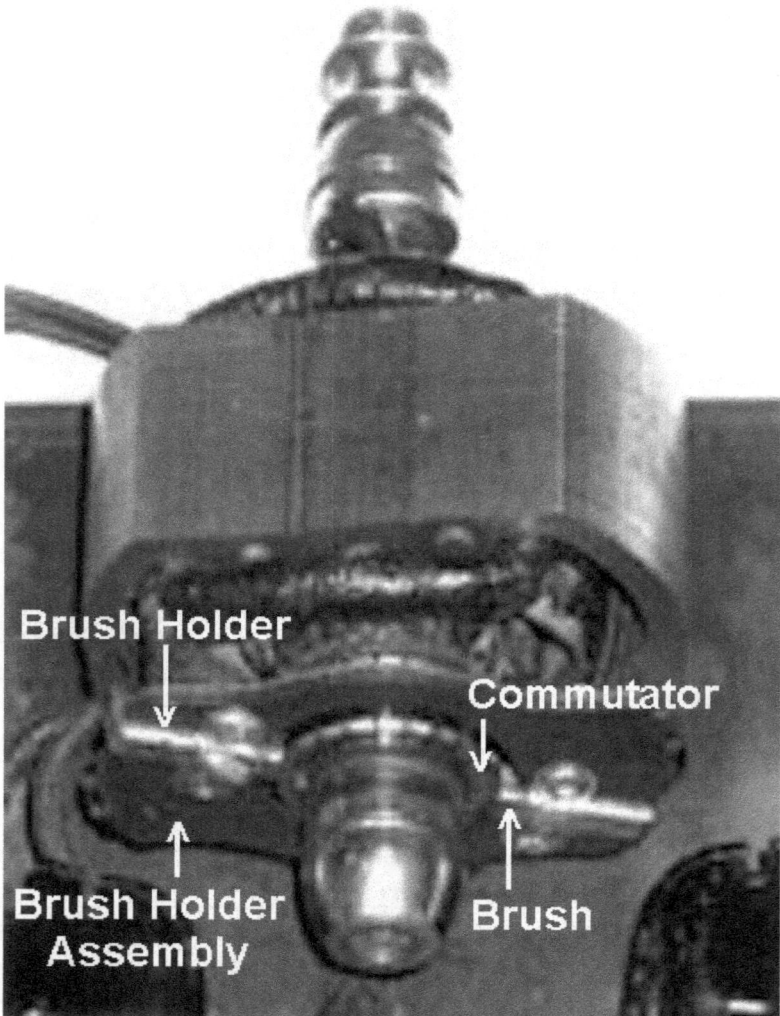

Brush Holder

Commutator

Brush Holder
Assembly

Brush

22. If you are replacing the carbon brushes, do one at a time. You must replace both.
23. Make sure that the carbon brush and spring assemblies easily move up and

down in their holders. <u>Do not use any type of lubricant or oil on these carbon brushes</u>.

24. While you have the motor apart, examine the commutator for shorted segments and excessive grooving.
25. Also look at each Bushing support assembly and ensure that they rotate freely. Clean the oil holes if they are plugged. Note that they have oil felt in them, and do not remove it from the holes.
26. Look for signs of overheating and any other damage. If all is OK, it is time to reassemble.

GE Motor Reassembly

Reassembly steps:

1. Carbon Brush and Spring assemblies are installed.
2. Carefully guide the commutator assembly thru the Motor winding Assembly.
3. Gently move the carbon Brushes back into their holders so the commutator assembly can be fully inserted.
4. Insure that the carbon brushes freely move on the commutator segment surface when finished adjusting.
5. Reinstall motor windings, commutator assembly and Brush Holder assembly in the bottom housing.
6. Ensure that Brush Holder assembly fits into grooves on each side of Bottom housing.
7. Position each Bushing Support assembly so that the oil hole is up.

8. Ensure that drive shaft rotates freely and does not bind.
9. Ensure that the wires are safely exiting the bottom housing.
10. Do one final inspection before installing the Top housing assembly.
11. The Top Housing assembly only goes on one way. The grooves in each side of the Top housing assembly must mate with the Fiber Brush Holder assembly. Do not Force!

Brush Holder Assembly Grooves

12. Gently install Top Housing assembly.
13. If necessary, press down evenly to get a snug fit. Do not hammer!
14. Ensure that shaft still rotates freely.
15. Carefully install the four screws thru the Top Housing into the Bottom Housing. Look

thru the end air holes if you have trouble lining up the screws.

16. Evenly tighten the four screws.

17. Ensure that shaft still rotates freely.
18. Put two drops of oil in each Bushing Support assembly oil hole. Rotate by hand and ensure that shaft still rotates freely.
19. Check drive shaft for excessive endplay by pulling out on shaft. There should only be a minimal amount of movement.
20. Plug Foot Pedal power cord into front 2-prong female connector.
21. Plug Main Power cord into rear input 2-prong mail connector.
22. Plug Main Power cord in to 120VAC power strip.
23. Slowly press down on Foot Pedal and power-up the drive motor.
24. Run motor slowly for a few minutes.

25. Watch for and listen for anything unusual, i.e. smoke, noise, etc. Immediately disconnect power if you suspect a problem. If there is a problem, I recommend that you take it to your Sewing Machine Technician or email me.
26. Do not run at full speed with no load as it is extremely bad for the motor.
27. Remove ALL POWER.
28. Disconnect all electrical cords.

29. Inspect the electrical wiring and connectors throughout the machine for deterioration and or damage. I have found that some of the wiring insulation in the oldest machines is now crumbling and exposing wires. Do not operate your machine if you find this. It will be a fire and shock hazard. Remember, these machines are NOT grounded.
30. If the wiring is OK and safe, continue.

31. Find the Mechanical Assembly, and carefully guide the Lamp Shade and Socket Assembly with its cable thru the top hole.
32. Let the non-motor end of the wooden base tilt farther down. This will let the motor pulley slide into the machine pulley hole.
33. Carefully fit the two assemblies together. Pay close attention to the front and rear connectors. They need to fit into their openings without damaging them. The connectors are old and brittle.
34. Once everything fits evenly together, install the five screws that you originally removed. Start with the center screw and then the corners.

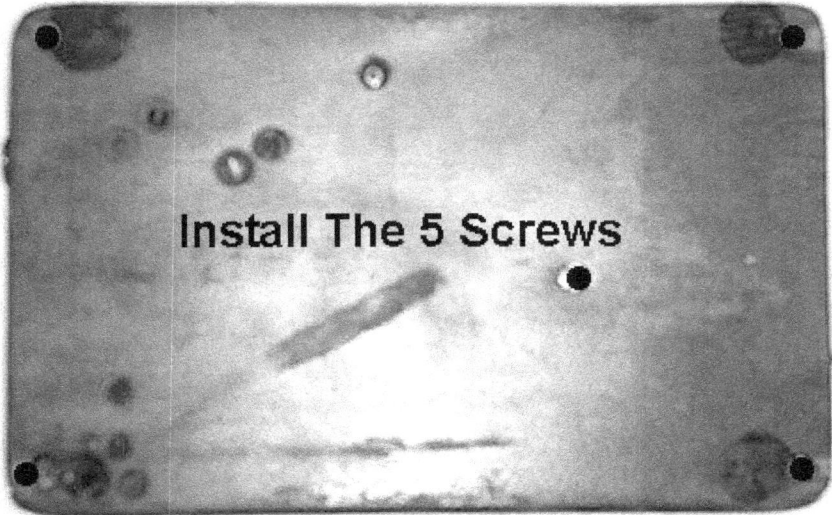

Install The 5 Screws

35. Do not tighten the screws, but check Bottom and Machine Assemblies for proper fit.

36. If satisfied, snug screws down, but do not over tighten.
37. Turn *Sewhandy* correct side up, and reinstall Lamp Shade and Socket Assembly with the two screws previously removed.

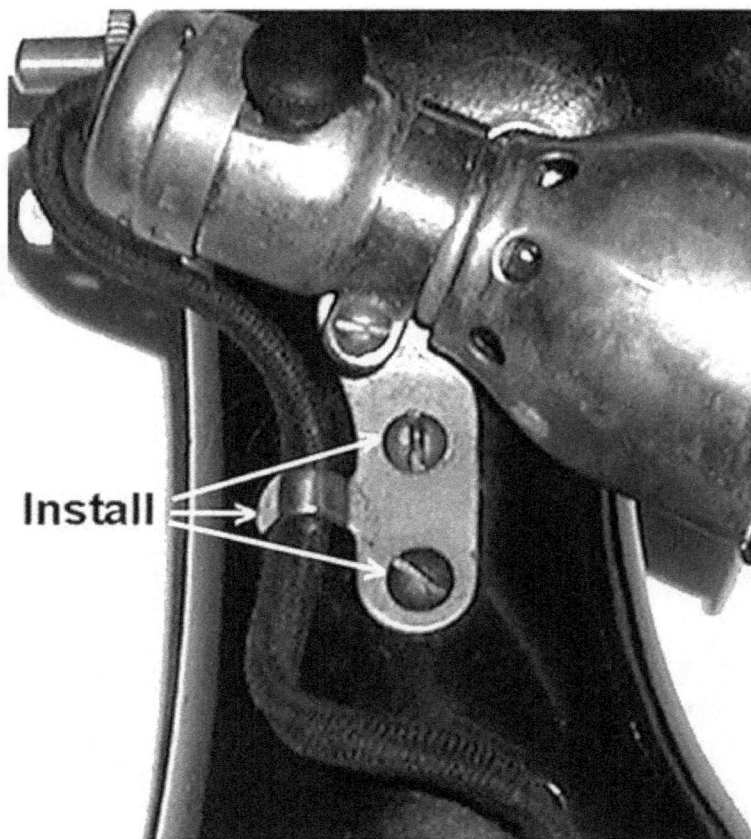

Install

38. Remove any cloth or towel from Spool Pin access hole. Check that nothing has gotten into the gears. While there, check that gears are lubricated. If not, lubricate with white lithium grease.

Remove Towel

39. Reinstall screws, Spool Pin and Plate.

Install

40. Reinstall drive belt.
41. Plug Foot Pedal power cord into front 2-prong female connector.
42. Plug Main Power cord into rear input 2-prong mail connector.
43. Plug Main Power cord in to 120VAC power strip.
44. <u>Slowly</u> press down on Foot Pedal and power-up the drive motor.
45. Run motor slowly for a few minutes.
46. Watch for and listen for anything unusual, i.e. smoke, noise, etc. Immediately disconnect power if you suspect a problem. If there is a problem, I recommend that you take to your Sewing Machine Technician or email me.
47. Perform a sewing check to ensure correct operation.

OSANN-SINGER Motor (BRK/BUK) Disassembly & Brush Replacement

Disassembly steps:

1. Remove ALL POWER.
2. Disconnect all electrical cords.
3. Remove the Drive belt.
4. Unscrew the two screws holding on the Lamp Shade and Socket Assembly. Gently lay it aside. (It will still be hooked to the electrical cable).

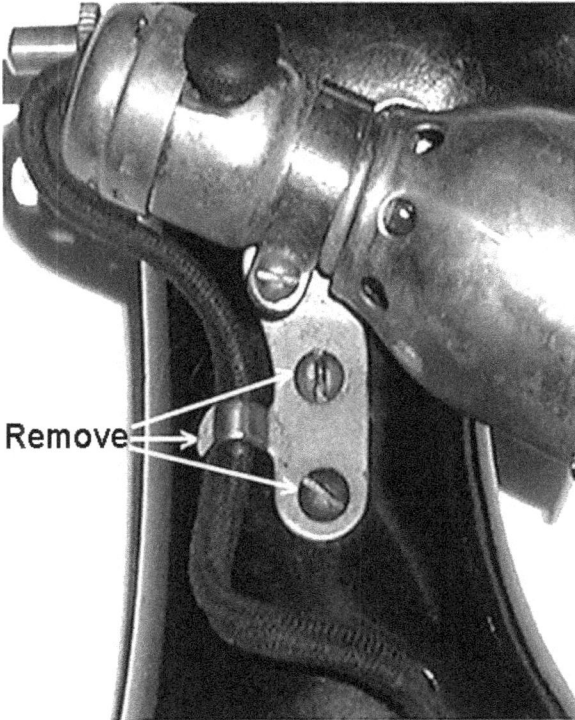

5. Remove the four screws holding on the Sewing Machine Motor nameplate.

6. Remove two screws holding Spool Pin and Plate. Remove Spool Pin and Plate.

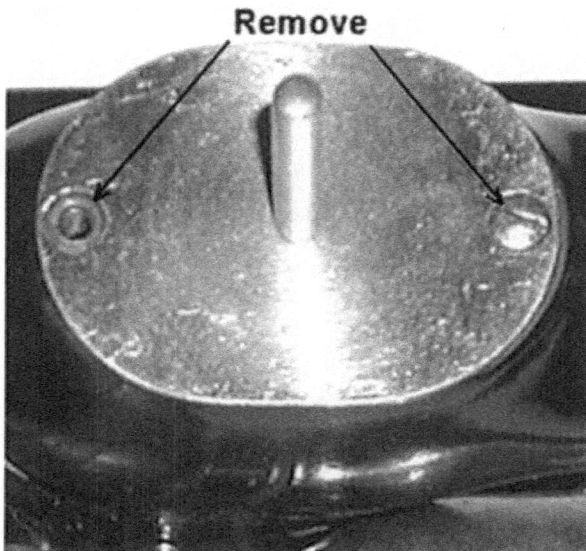

7. Insert small piece of cloth or towel into the access hole to keep anything else from getting to the gears.

Insert Towel

8. Gently turn *Sewhandy* over so that you are looking at the wooden bottom.
9. <u>Only remove the FIVE screws</u> that I have indicated in following the picture. Removal of the other screws will make everything much more difficult.

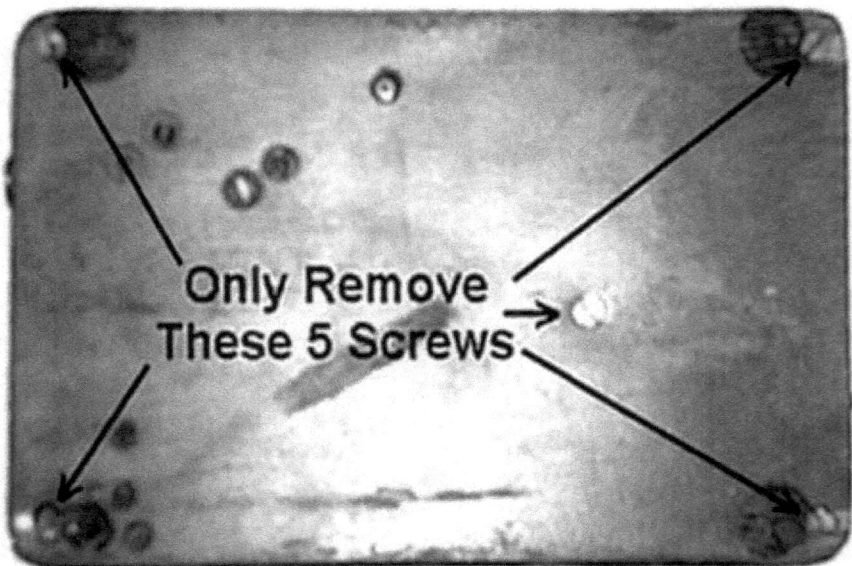

Only Remove
These 5 Screws

10. While holding the neck of the *Sewhandy* in one hand and supporting the wooden base with the other hand, slowly lift the two assemblies apart.
11. Let the non-motor end of the wooden base tilt farther down. This will let the motor pulley slide though the machine hole.
12. Carefully guide the Sewing Machine Motor nameplate and the Lamp Shade and Socket Assembly with its cable thru the top hole.
13. You now have two separate parts: The sewing machine Mechanical assembly, and the Bottom Electrical assembly. Set the Mechanical assembly safely aside.

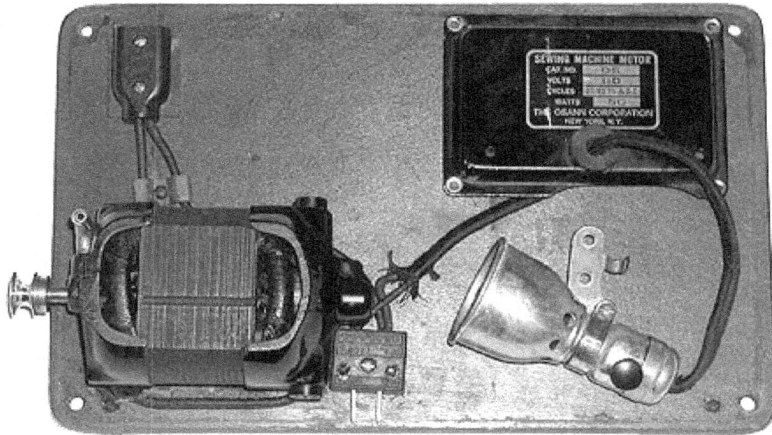

14. Note that there are two **ASBESTOS** spacer pads underneath the bottom of the motor. **DO NOT DISTURB** them.

Asbestos Spacers

15. This is a **SINGER BRK/BUK** series motor (without the label). The carbon brushes

**are replaced the same way they are on the
SINGER Model 221 Featherweight motor.**

16. On the non-pulley end of either side of the
    motor there is a black plastic Brush
    Retaining Screw. Gently remove the screw,
    and the carbon brush and spring assembly
    can be removed for replacement.

    <u>Only take one carbon Brush and Spring
    assembly out at a time, and note the exact
    position of the carbon brush in its holder</u>.
    This will allow you to correctly reinstall the
    carbon brush if it is not necessary to
    replace it. Pay special attention to the
    position of the concave end in relation to
    the commutator segments contact surface.

Brush Screws

17. If you are replacing the carbon brushes, do one at a time. You cannot replace just one brush, must replace both.
18. Make sure that the carbon brush and spring assemblies easily move up and down in their holders. Do not use any type of lubricant or oil on these carbon brushes.
19. Reinstall the Brush Screws.
20. Also look at the Bushing support at each motor end and ensure that they motor lubricant tube and holes are not plugged.
21. Look for signs of motor overheating and any other damage. If all is OK, it is time to reassemble.

OSANN-SINGER Motor Reassembly

Reassembly steps:

1. Carbon Brush and Spring assemblies are installed.
2. SINGER Motors do not use oil for lubrication. Per SINGER, only use SINGER Motor Lubricant (Grease) in the motors. Insert lubricant as needed in the Grease Tubes. Rotate by hand and ensure that shaft rotates freely.

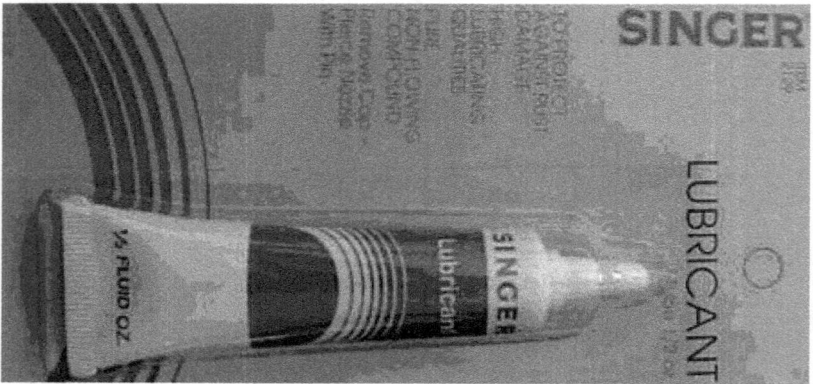

3. Check drive shaft for excessive endplay by pulling out on shaft. There should only be a minimal amount of movement.
4. Plug Foot pedal power cord into front 2-prong female connector.
5. Plug Main Power cord into rear input 2-prong mail connector.
6. Plug Main Power cord in to 120VAC power strip.

7. **Slowly** press down on Foot Pedal and power-up the drive motor.
8. Run motor slowly for a few minutes.
9. Watch for and listen for anything unusual, i.e. smoke, noise, etc. Immediately disconnect power if you suspect a problem. If there is a problem, I recommend that you take it to your Sewing Machine Technician or email me.
10. Do not run at full speed with no load as it is extremely bad for the motor.
11. Remove ALL POWER.
12. Disconnect all electrical cords.

13. Inspect the electrical wiring and connectors throughout the machine for deterioration and or damage. I have found that some of the wiring insulation in the oldest machines is now crumbling and exposing wires. Do not operate your

machine if you find this. It will be a fire and shock hazard. Remember, these machines are NOT grounded.

14. If the wiring is OK and safe, continue.
15. Find the Mechanical Assembly, and carefully guide the Sewing Machine Motor nameplate and the Lamp Shade and Socket Assembly with its cable thru the top hole.
16. Let the non-motor end of the wooden base tilt farther down. This will let the motor pulley slide into the machine pulley hole.
17. Carefully fit the two assemblies together. Pay close attention to the front and rear connectors. They need to fit into their openings without damaging them. The connectors are old and brittle.
18. Once everything fits evenly together, install the five screws that you originally removed. Start with the center screw and then the corners.

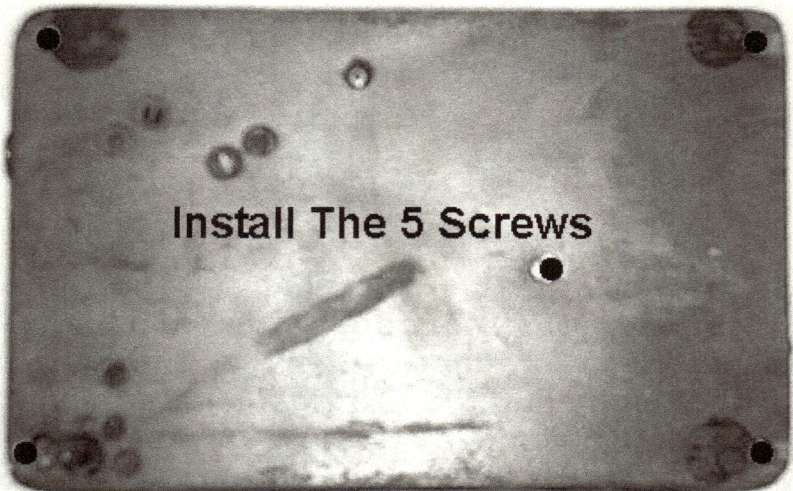

Install The 5 Screws

19. Do not tighten the screws, but check Bottom and Machine Assemblies for proper fit.
20. If satisfied, snug screws down, but do not over tighten.
21. Turn machine correct side up, and reinstall the Lamp Shade and Socket Assembly with the two screws previously removed.

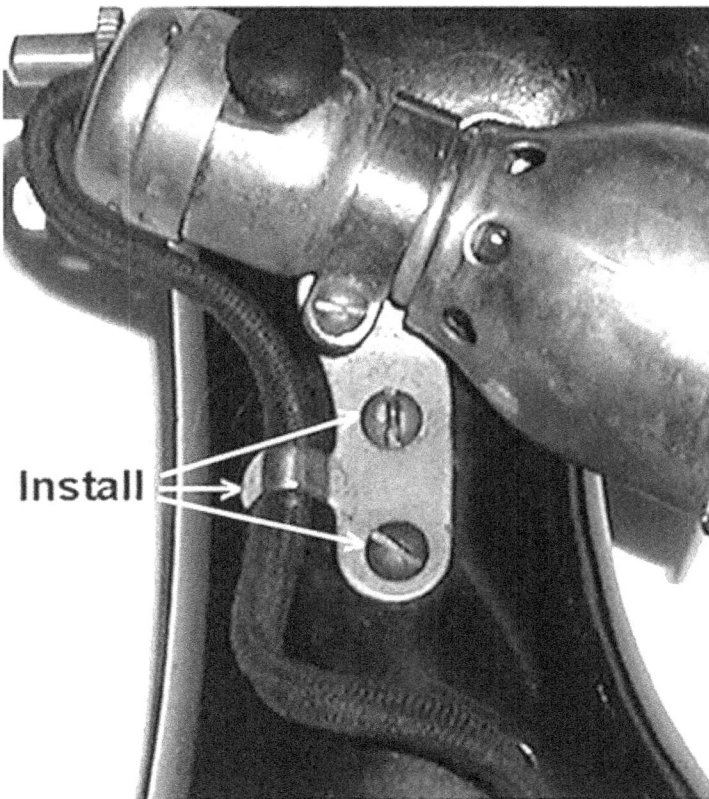

Install

22. Reinstall the four screws and the Sewing Machine motor nameplate.

Install the Screws

23. **Remove any cloth or towel from Spool Pin access hole. Check that nothing has gotten into the gears. While there, check that gears are lubricated. If not lubricate with white lithium grease.**

Remove Towel

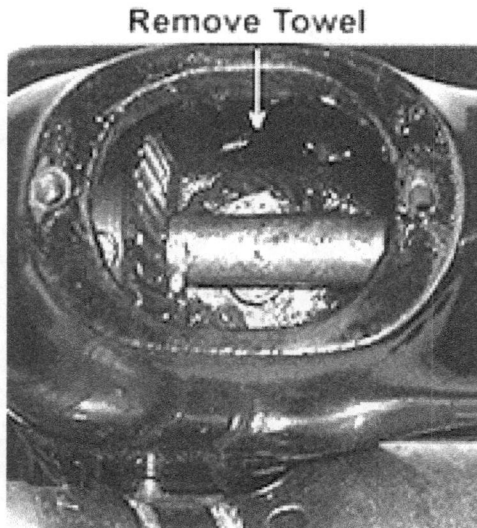

24. **Reinstall the two screws and the Spool Pin and Plate.**

164

Install

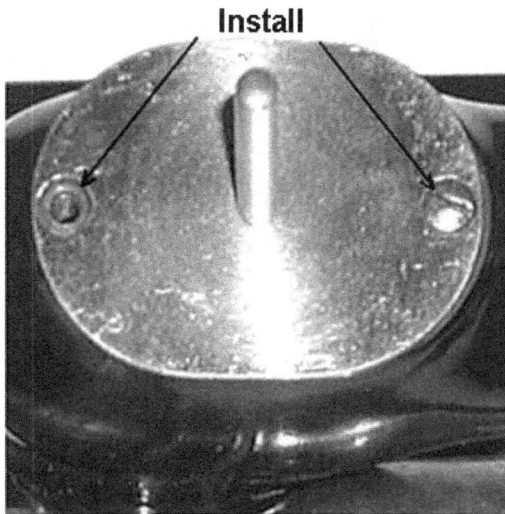

25. Reinstall drive belt.
26. Plug Foot Pedal power cord into front 2-prong female connector.
27. Plug Main Power cord into rear input 2-prong mail connector.
28. Plug Main Power cord in to 120VAC power strip.
29. <u>Slowly</u> press down on Foot Pedal and power drive motor.
30. Run motor slowly for a few minutes.
31. Watch for and listen for anything unusual, i.e. smoke, noise, etc. Immediately disconnect power if you suspect a problem. If there is a problem, I recommend that you take it to your Sewing Machine Technician or email me.
32. Perform a sewing check to ensure correct operation.

Form K3691

INSTRUCTIONS

FOR USING AND ADJUSTING

SINGER

B.U.K. ELECTRIC MOTORS

WITH FOOT CONTROLLER FOR
FAMILY SEWING MACHINES

When requiring
Needles, Oil,
Parts or Repairs
for your Machine

Look for the
Red "S"
There are Singer
Shops in every City

THE SINGER MANUFACTURING CO.

1931

SINGER B.U.K Electric Motor Book

TROUBLESHOOTING & REPAIR

Before I get to the actual troubleshooting and repair, I need to cover safety in troubleshooting

Safety

Most people have a fear of electricity. Over the years, the public safety messages, our teachers, parents, and friends have pounded into our heads how dangerous electricity is, and how you will probably die if you get anywhere near it. I know people that are afraid to change their own light bulbs.

Some of the warnings are true... Electricity can kill, just as a car will kill if used improperly. Or just as something as simple as a knife, if used incorrectly, may cause you to cut yourself and quickly bleed to death. There are rules to follow for cars, knives, and for electricity. All of these items require you recognize and be aware of the dangers and risk, and their proper safe handling procedures. Electricity will cause fatal burns or make vital organs in your body no longer work properly if you make a fatal mistake.

Most people have experienced a tingle when exposed to electricity. Many of you have experienced the discomfort caused by the group joker sliding his feet on the carpet to build up static, and then touching your ear. Obviously, it

167

does not take much of a shock for us to take notice.

Generally, a current of five mA (milliamps) or less will cause a shock sensation, but will rarely cause any damage. Larger currents can cause muscle contraction. Currents as low as 100 mA for even a few seconds can be fatal depending on the voltage and how and where they pass through your body.

That ever-present 110/120VAC home wall socket circuit is capable of 15 to 20 Amps (15000 to 20000 mA). Fifteen to Twenty Thousand mA is 150 to 200 times the possibly fatal 100 mA mentioned in the above paragraph. OK, this is an extreme example. If it were always true, most of us would already be dead.

The most important concept is:

DO
NOT
EVER
ALLOW
YOURSELF
TO BECOME
THE GROUND
RETURN PATH!

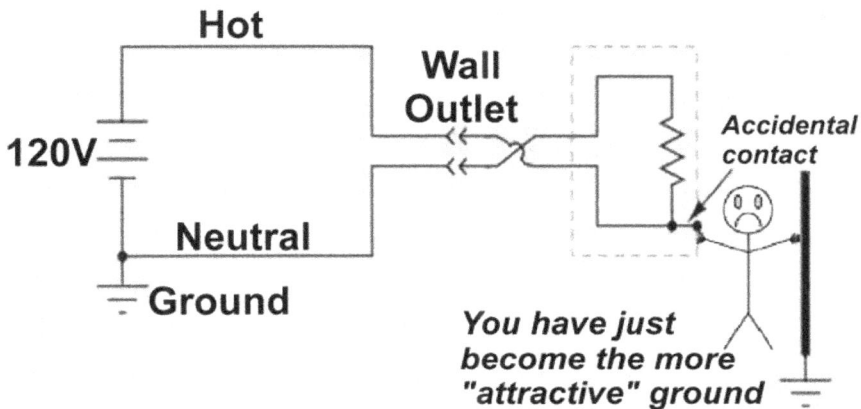

Hot

Wall
Outlet

120V

Neutral

Ground

Accidental contact

You have just become the more "attractive" ground

Electricity will follow the most attractive ground it finds. One of the basic rules of electricity is that <u>current follows the path of least resistance</u>.

If you and your body are more attractive (the path of least resistance) to the electricity then the previous ground path that it was using, then you will quickly become a <u>new part of the circuit and the new ground return path</u>. Refer to the illustration above and on the next page.

Luckily, in our modern homes with 120VAC wall outlets, smart safety officials have mandated that "Ground Fault Circuit Interrupters" or GFCIs be installed in the house circuits. The basic protection that these provide is that if you do accidentally become a more attractive Ground Return Path, the GFCI will sense that

and cut the circuit in microseconds. This usually prevents electrocution.

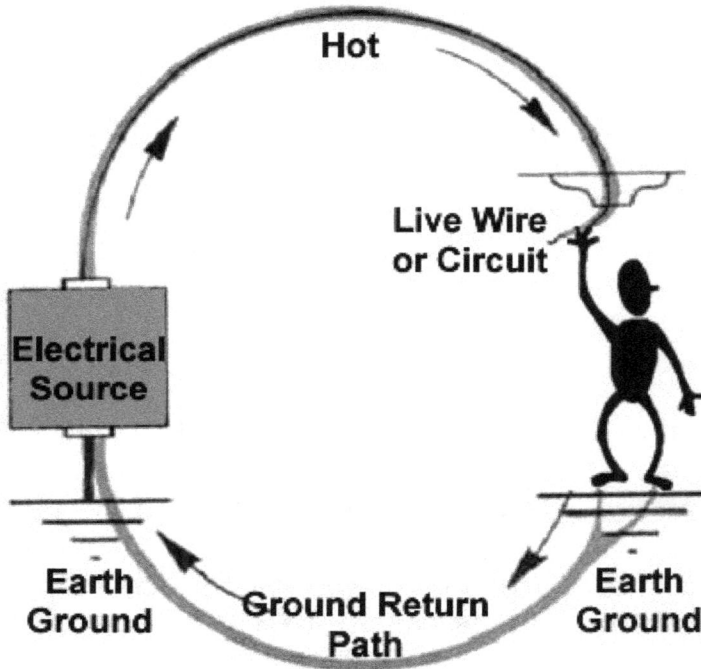

However, do not disregard common-sense safety practices and depend on the GFCI to keep you from being shocked. Like all things, a GFCI can fail with the result that you might again become a <u>new part of the circuit and the more attractive ground return path</u>.

At all possible times, troubleshooting should be performed with all power disconnected. This means that you should <u>personally ensure</u> that all

the power is disconnected, and that the power remains off while you are working on the circuits You could always have someone else check, but how important is this to him? I mean it is your life at risk, not his...

However, sometimes troubleshooting with the power off is not possible and there is no option but to troubleshoot with the power on. Do this only as a last resort, and be aware that you have just <u>numerically multiplied</u> your risk of being injured.

Think about it and ask yourself, is this the only way to troubleshoot the circuit, and is finding the problem worth losing your life? Or is doing it with power on just quicker and easier? Your Headstone might read something like this:

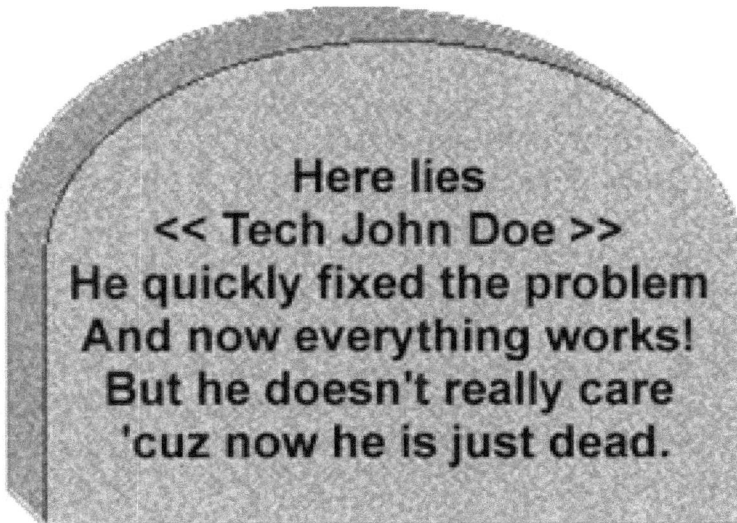

Here lies
<< Tech John Doe >>
He quickly fixed the problem
And now everything works!
But he doesn't really care
'cuz now he is just dead.

Another common sense safety practice that most of us *IGNORE* is that we must always remove all articles of clothing or jewelry that could be conductive when working near energized parts. Why anyone would wear jewelry when working on parts, electrical or not, makes no sense to me. Jewelry is way too expensive to damage.

Over the years I have learned a number of rules that helped me avoid electrical shocks. First, approach every electrical circuit as if it is powered. Even if you personally disconnected the power, <u>always treat the circuit as if it has power on it</u>.

Another rule is to keep my left hand in my left rear pocket while troubleshooting. I am right-handed so this works fine. If you are left-handed, just apply this to your right hand. In any case, with my left hand in my left rear pocket, it would be impossible for me to make the "ultimate fatal mistake" of making a Ground Return path from my right hand to my left hand.

I call this situation the "ultimate fatal mistake" because the circuit path in your body goes right through your heart. Since your heart beat depends upon your body's internal electrical stimulation, exposure of your heart muscle to a much stronger outside electrical source is usually fatal.

The more scientific description of this would be that during the Ventricular Relaxation period of the normal heart cycle, the heart is most vulnerable to an external high current pulse.

Here are the above rules, along with some others:

1) Do not allow yourself to become the Ground Return Path!

2) All troubleshooting should be performed with all power off!

3) Personally turn-off, mark, and lock power off!

4) Approach all circuits as if they are powered!

5) Verify by test that the power is <u>OFF</u>. Test occasionally to ensure that power is still off.

6) Keep your other hand in your rear pocket in order to prevent any chance of making a Ground Return Path through your heart.

7) Any time you are working on or with electricity, appliances, or components, always expect the unexpected!

Meter Safety

In addition to rules for your personal safety, there are also safety rules that apply to the use of diagnostic and troubleshooting tools.

Electrical measuring tools or meters (voltmeters, ohmmeters, ammeters, and multimeters) are indispensable aids in your troubleshooting. Safe and efficient use of test meters is an extremely valuable skill for anyone contemplating electrical repair.

This is both for the sake of your own personal safety and for the continued operation of the measuring tool. Carelessness is the greatest factor when both experienced and beginner technicians have electrical accidents.

All meters have probes with conductive tips on long wires to allow measurement of electrical signals. It is an _absolute rule_ that you do not let the conductive probe tips touch one another when they are both in contact with different test points or voltage levels in a circuit.

If this happens on a non-powered circuit where you are performing resistance or continuity checks, then your measurements will be wrong. If you do not notice your mistake, your later troubleshooting may be also be faulty and lead you down the wrong troubleshooting path.

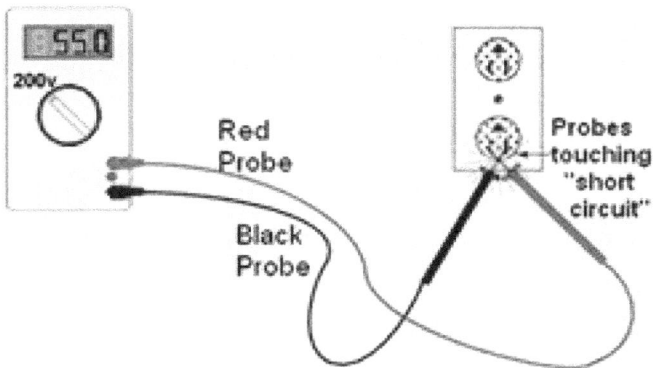

If this happens on a powered circuit with two points of different potential, you will immediately have a short-circuit. Your first sign will be a spark and perhaps even a ball of flame if the voltage source is capable of supplying enough current!

Consider each meter to be unique. Just because you "know" one meter does not mean you can safely operate another. Actually read and understand the meter operation manual. Pay attention to the meter specifications and signal limits. Practice with your Meter until you know how to correctly and safely use it.

Make sure your meter is still working correctly as you troubleshoot. Example: An analog needle meter will show zero when it is dead... What if you base your next step on that zero reading? A digital will not show a LCD reading if it is dead, but it sure will show zero if the input lead fuse is blown.

Do not attempt to measure more current than the meter can safely handle (usually around 10 Amps, but each meter is different.) Do not attempt to measure resistance on a "live" or powered circuit (least – blown fuse, worst – Meter death.) Do not exceed the Meter AC and DC Voltage limits.

An inexpensive meter may be all you need. Buying an expensive one with all sorts of options that you may never use is not practical. And when you drop it, or burn it up, or leave it in a hot car (and you will) and it dies.... You will not feel as bad losing one that cost you only twenty dollars.

Do not hold the meter probes by the metal tips or use probes that appear to have bad insulation (shocking experience.) And last...

<u>Do not ever become the</u>
<u>GROUND RETURN PATH</u>

What is Troubleshooting?

Troubleshooting is the act of pinpointing and correcting problems in any kind of system. A sewing machine technician uses troubleshooting and observations of the machines behavior to decide his approach and to determine and repair the problems.

A doctor does the same with his patients. He observes both the patient and test results to troubleshoot the problem cause. We actually say he is diagnosing the patient and prescribing a cure.

Think of this as Detective or Crime Scene Investigation (CSI) work. Instead of looking for clues to catch the "bad guy", you are looking for clues to catch the "bad cause." OK, it does not sound as cool as being a CSI person, but the theory is the same. Whatever you call it, it is still finding the cause.

Troubleshooters must be able to find the cause or causes of a problem by examining or observing its effects. Often, multiple conflicting and seemingly unrelated observations mask the actual fault source.

Cause and effect relationships are often complex, even for simple systems. An experienced and competent troubleshooter has the ability to identify the root cause of a problem quickly.

Some people seem to be born with a natural talent for troubleshooting; however, it is a skill to learn like any other with continued practice.

Sometimes the system to be fault diagnosed is in so bad a condition that there is no logical place to start. In this case, it might be better to just "throw in the towel" and replace it with a new one. Economics and available time will be a big part of that decision.

Usually though, a system is still partially working so that its operation may be tested and adjusted by the troubleshooter as part of a diagnostic procedure.

Here troubleshooting follows the scientific method: determining cause/effect relationships by means of live experimentation.

The scientific method has four steps:
1. Observation and description of a phenomenon or group of phenomena.
2. Formulation of a hypothesis to explain the phenomena.
3. Use of the hypothesis to predict the existence of other phenomena, or to predict quantitatively the results of new observations.
4. Performance of experimental tests of the predictions by properly performed experiments.

My troubleshooting method has similar steps, but I have added a few more to make the process clear:
1. Observation of the system operation and faults.
2. Clearly understand the problem.
3. Gather any additional information.
4. Isolate the problem from everything else.

5. Come up with/formulate/hypothesize a cause or causes to explain the fault observation.
6. Use of the cause or causes to determine the probability of its effect and other expected observations.
7. Performance of experimental tests to determine validity of your suspected cause(s).

The seven steps above will help you come up with answers to the following questions:
1. What actually is the problem?
2. What indicates there is a problem?
3. Is there really a problem?
4. When did this problem occur?
5. What are the possible causes?
6. What is the most probable cause?
7. What is the second, third, fourth, fifth, etc most probable cause?
8. Where do you start your troubleshooting?
9. Which tool(s) should you use to perform the troubleshooting?

Remember the Detective and CSI analogy. You are investigating and looking at everything for clues as to the cause of the fault(s).

Once you find the cause, you are only half done. You still have to fix the problem. Sometimes that is as simple as reseating or removing corrosion from a connector, other times it may require component replacement.

While troubleshooting follows rules, it is actually a mixture of those rules and personal creativity. During your troubleshooting, you may have to invent your own specific technique adapted to that specific system you are working on. Be creative in examining a problem from different perspectives or angles. Ask different questions when the "standard" questions do not lead to fruitful answers. Some call this "thinking outside the box."

The Flashlight Exercise

This exercise in thinking "out of the box" uses the typical home two D cell battery flashlight. First, list all the problems that can keep the flashlight from lighting up (try for at least 30).

This might be easier if you grab a flashlight and look at it. Next, prioritize your list according to probability with the most likely first.

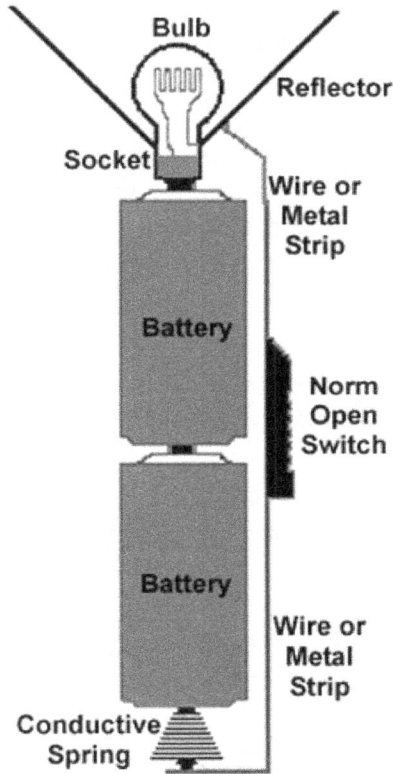

Bulb

Reflector

Socket

Wire or
Metal
Strip

Battery

Norm
Open
Switch

Battery

Wire or
Metal
Strip

Conductive
Spring

Most people will put "battery" as the very first one on the list. That is a good answer, but we need to be more exact in the failure. Use specific terms like "battery dead," or "battery corroded" or "wrong type battery" for the list.

Here is my list (random probability):
1. battery dead
2. battery missing
3. battery corroded
4. battery wrong type
5. battery installed incorrectly

6. battery contacts bent
7. battery contacts missing
8. battery contacts corroded
9. tension spring missing
10. tension spring corroded
11. tension spring – no tension
12. bulb burned out
13. bulb broken
14. bulb missing
15. bulb wrong type
16. bulb installed incorrectly
17. bulb bottom contact flattened
18. bulb socket loose
19. bulb socket missing
20. bulb socket corroded
21. bulb socket cross-threaded
22. bulb socket contact corroded
23. bulb socket contact bent
24. bulb socket contact missing
25. switch bad – open
26. switch bad – shorted
27. switch corroded
28. switch missing
29. ground wire to switch corroded
30. ground wire to switch open
31. ground wire to switch missing
32. wire switch to bulb socket open
33. wire switch to bulb socket corroded
34. wire switch to bulb socket shorted
35. wire switch to bulb socket missing

Next put your list in order of the most to least probable faults. Compare your list with mine.

Here is my list according to probability:
1. battery dead
2. battery missing
3. bulb burned out
4. bulb broken
5. bulb missing
6. battery installed incorrectly
7. battery wrong type
8. battery corroded
9. battery contacts corroded
10. battery contacts bent
11. tension spring corroded
12. tension spring – no tension
13. battery contacts missing
14. tension spring missing
15. bulb installed incorrectly
16. bulb bottom contact flattened
17. bulb wrong type
18. bulb socket loose
19. bulb socket corroded
20. bulb socket missing
21. bulb socket cross-threaded
22. bulb socket contact bent
23. bulb socket contact corroded
24. bulb socket contact missing
25. switch bad – open
26. switch bad – shorted
27. switch corroded
28. switch missing
29. ground wire to switch corroded
30. ground wire to switch open
31. ground wire to switch missing
32. wire switch to bulb socket open
33. wire switch to bulb socket corroded

34. wire switch to bulb socket shorted
35. wire switch to bulb socket missing

Which would you tackle first? Would it be the most probable, the easiest to check, or maybe a combination of both?

Anything with the batteries would be my first choice. Corrosion would be easy to find with a visual check of all parts, and would eliminate many of the possibilities.

So what good was this exercise? The flashlight has most of the components of larger more complex systems. If one flashlight has at least 30 possible faults, just think how many electrical fault possibilities there are for a modern sewing machine.

Remember that no matter how large or complex the system, the approach to troubleshooting is the same whether it is a *Sewhandy* or a computer-controlled embroidery machine.

Sewhandy
TROUBLESHOOTING

This section discusses *Sewhandy* common failures and their probable causes. I have listed 86 faults. Look for your failure in the alphabetical list below. Remember the flashlight exercise... not all the possible faults or causes are listed here.

1. Balls under throat plate:

Thread balls happen with **ALL MACHINES**. Causes can be as simple as not correctly pulling the bottom thread before starting, or loading the bobbin wrong. Other causes are incorrect thread tension (top and bottom), bent needle, damaged bobbin case and hook, and incorrect timing.

The very first things to do are to open the Slide Plate and to remove the needle, needle plate, bobbin and bobbin case. Clean the whole area of lint and dust. Check the hook for any signs of visible damage. If there is any damage, blend out the damage with a rubberized brush strip.

Check the needle for straightness. Install the needle and manually rotate it up and down to check for contact with the hook. Check that the hook passes slightly above the needle eye as the needle is rising with the normal machine rotation. Adjust timing as required. See the Chapter on Timing on page 227.

Check that the bobbin is correctly filled. Check the bobbin case for any damage. Install the bobbin into the bobbin case correctly and check for rotation.

Check for the correct thread tension coming out of the bobbin case. If it is wrong, adjust the spring tension. See the Chapter on Tension on page 217.

Install the bobbin and bobbin case into the *Sewhandy* hook. Manually rotate the needle up and down to check for contact with the bobbin case. Note: If the needle is not installed correctly (all the way to the top) or if the needle is the wrong type (see Replaceable Consumables) it will hit the bobbin case and will quickly damage the needle point. If everything is OK, engage the bobbin case retainer. Add a drop of oil to the hook and bobbin case contact surface. Reinstall the needle plate, and close the slide plate.

Check the top thread path and tension for even flow and tension. Adjust as necessary. Thread needle, bring bottom thread up, and manually sew a few stitches before machine sewing.

2. Belt slips – Belt old – Belt wrong:

All belts get old, and either wear out or deteriorate. Exposure to oils can make this happen faster. Look for cracks or cuts. Usually, a belt problem is because you have the wrong belt installed on the *Sewhandy*. I have seen everything from rubber bands to Featherweight toothed belt installed on them. See the Chapter on Replacing Consumables on page 235 for more information on the correct belt.

If the belt is too loose it becomes frustrating, but if the belt is too tight you run the chance of wearing out either (or both) the Hook Shaft bushing or the Motor bushing.

Belts occasionally dry out. You can use some soap on the belt to quiet it, but DO NOT EVER USE ANY OIL or ANY PETROLEUM PRODUCT on the belt as they will ruin the belt.

3. Belt Wheel problems, Belt Wheel Locked: See Hand Wheel problems, Hand Wheel Locked.

4. Bobbin case chewed up: This is caused by either the bobbin case being installed incorrectly, the needle is bent, or the machine timing is wrong. See the Chapter on Timing on page 227.

5. Bobbin case falls out : The bobbin case retainer should latch to keep this from happening. Check latch operation.

6. Bobbin case jammed: Occasionally, so much thread and junk gets caught up in the bobbin case, hook, needle, and feed dogs that

everything jams. First, cut the thread and remove the needle. Open the slide plate, and remove the throat plate. Manually move the hook and feed dogs back and forth, and cut and remove any binding thread. This should free everything up. Correctly reinstall all the parts. Add a drop of oil to the hook and bobbin case contact surface. Check the top thread path and tension for even flow and tension. Adjust as necessary. Thread needle, bring bottom thread up, and manually sew a few stitches before machine sewing.

7. Bobbin case loose: The bobbin case locating projections must fit in the hook locating indentation. Normally, the bobbin case retainer will not latch closed unless the bobbin case is correctly installed. Check the position and operation of both. Note: If the four screws that hold the bobbin case retainer are loose than the retainer will not hold the bobbin case in the hook. DO NOT OVERTIGHTEN THE FOUR SCREWS – They will strip.

8. Bobbin tension intermittent: See the Chapter on Tension on page 217.

9. Bobbin tension will not adjust: See the Chapter on Tension on page 217.

10. Bottom tension wrong: See the Chapter on Tension on page 217.

11. Bobbin thread not being brought
up: Check that the needle is installed correctly (all the way to the top and flat side to the right). Check bobbin case threading. Check the hook timing (see the Chapter on Timing on page 227).

12. Electrical wiring and insulation
disintegrating: This is very common on older machines and presents an extreme electrical hazard. The *Sewhandy* uses an insulated, non-polarized and non-grounded, electrical system just like most other vintage sewing machines (including the SINGER Featherweight Models 221 and 222).

If the insulation completely breaks down, the sewing machine chassis will be electrically "HOT". Replace the wiring if there is any doubt as to its safety. Replacement wire is listed in the Chapter on Replacing Consumables on page 235.

13. Feed Dogs are not moving: The
Sewhandy Feed Dogs are completely mechanical. If they are not moving, then there is something wrong with the Feed mechanism, the Feed Shaft gear, or the Hook Shaft Spur gear. Read pages 88 – 94 for the theory. Compare the pictures with your machine. Email me with questions at <u>Dar-Bet@att.net</u> .

14. Feed Dogs are not moving
fabric: Check that the Feed Dogs move at all.

If they do, they may be too worn to pull the fabric back. Check that they rise above the Needle Plate. Check for lint in the Feed Dogs. The Pressor Foot pressure may be either too low (allowing the Feed Dogs to slip under the fabric) or too high (seizing the fabric between the Feed Dogs and Pressor Foot bottom). Adjust the pressure as necessary for best operation.

The Feed Dog timing may be incorrect. See the Chapter on Timing on page 227 for more information.

15. Feed Dogs worn: Usually, worn Feed Dogs are a result of running the machine with the Pressor Foot down and with no fabric between the Feed Dogs and the Pressor Foot. This grinds down the Feed Dog upper teeth surface against Pressor Foot. Make sure the Feed Dog teeth rise above the Needle Plate. Worn-out Feed Dogs can be repaired or replaced. Email me at **Dar-Bet@att.net** .

16. Foot pedal does not vary from full speed: This is caused by a problem with the Foot Pedal itself. Terminal 20 and Finger 20 are shorted together. It is very important to remember that this is a non-polarized and an ungrounded system. The design of the interior of the Foot Pedal is such that the outer case is insulated from the Hot side. However, if the insulation were to be disturbed and fail, then there is a strong chance of electrical shock.

Refer to pages 105 - 111 for wiring diagram and Foot Pedal theory of operation.

17. Foot pedal does not vary from half or slow speed: This is caused by a problem with the Foot Pedal itself. One of the Resistive Terminals (15 – 19) and its associated Finger (15 – 19) are shorted together. It is very important to remember that this is a non-polarized and an ungrounded system.

The design of the interior of the Foot Pedal is such that the outer case is insulated from the *Hot* side. However, if the insulation were to be disturbed and fail, then there is a strong chance of electrical shock. Refer to pages 105 - 111 for wiring diagram and Foot Pedal theory of operation.

18. Foot pedal hot or smokes: Stop using the Foot Pedal immediately! Your Foot Pedal MUST NEVER get hot or smoke. It is very important to remember that this is a non-polarized and an ungrounded system. The design of the interior of the Foot Pedal is such that the outer case is insulated from the *Hot* (Power) side.

If the insulation breaks down and fails there is a strong chance of electrical shock. Refer to pages 105 - 111 for wiring diagram and Foot Pedal theory of operation. However, I strongly recommend that you have a professional sewing machine technician perform the troubleshooting and/or repair. I can provide this thru www.SewingMachineTech.com.

19. Foot pedal inop (does nothing):

This may be caused by a problem with the Foot Pedal front connector, the Foot Pedal itself, *Sewhandy* internal wiring, the Main Power rear connector, the motor, or the *Sewhandy* to 120VAC power cord. With everything plugged in correctly, try to turn the light on. If it lights (assuming the bulb is good), then you can eliminate some of the possible causes.

It is very important to remember that this is a non-polarized and an ungrounded system. The design of the interior of the Foot Pedal is such that the outer case is insulated from the *Hot* side. However, if the insulation were to be disturbed and fail, then there is a strong chance of electrical shock. Refer to pages 105 - 111 for wiring diagram and Foot Pedal theory of operation.

20. Foot pedal not plugged in, yet machine runs: This is caused by a short between the two conductors in the *Sewhandy* internal wiring for the Foot Pedal circuit. It is very important to remember that this is a non-polarized and an ungrounded system. Refer to pages 105 - 111 for wiring diagram and Foot Pedal theory of operation.

192

21. Hand wheel hard to turn: This usually indicates that the belt tension is too tight. While it does make it harder to turn the hand wheel, the real problem is that it places excessive load on the machine bearings and will shorten the life of the motor and bearings. It may also be a lack of lubrication. See the Chapter on Lubrication on page 127.

22. Hand Wheel problems, Hand Wheel Locked: A hand/belt wheel that is locked is usually the result of a gearing problem in the *Sewhandy*. To determine if this is the problem, just take the belt off and try to turn the hand wheel. It should move easily, if not check the shuttle hook and feed dog drive path, and the needle drive path for gear hang-ups – See Locked.

Hand wheels are important. Sure, they give you a place to grab to manually move the needle. More importantly hand wheels are to sewing machine as flywheels are to automobiles. Both smooth-out any changes or pulse in the rotational movement. If the hand wheel is incorrectly mounted or loose, it will intermittently unbalance the *Sewhandy*.

23. Hitting something: This is usually the result of a timing problem with the needle hitting the hook. Check the *Sewhandy* timing. Install the needle and manually rotate it up and down to check for contact with the hook. Check that the hook passes just above the needle eye as the needle is rising with the normal machine rotation. Adjust the timing as required. See the Chapter on Timing on page 227 for more information.

Hitting something also can occur after you have serviced your *Sewhandy* and either left something loose, or left a tool, i.e. small screwdriver, inside the *Sewhandy*.

24. Hook not rotating (machine not jammed): Read pages 88 - 94 for theory of operation. The Hook is loose on the Hook Shaft. Tighten the two small screws- DO NOT OVERTIGHTEN. You must retime the *Sewhandy*. Do not attempt to sew without checking the timing. See the Chapter on Timing on page 227.

25. Installing the Needle: The 15x1 needle must be installed all the way to the top with the Flat side of the needle facing toward the right side of the *Sewhandy*. This is exactly opposite the SINGER Featherweight which faces the Flat to the left. See Needles on page 204..

26. Intermittent operation: This is an electrical problem. It could be anywhere in the electrical system. It is very important to remember that this is a non-polarized and an ungrounded system. For troubleshooting help, refer to the Chapter on Electrical Operation on

page 95 for theory of operation and wiring diagrams.

27. Knocking sound: This is usually the result of a timing problem with the needle hitting the hook. Check the *Sewhandy* timing. Install the needle and manually rotate it up and down to check for contact with the hook. Check that the hook passes just above the needle eye as the needle is rising with the normal machine rotation. Adjust timing as required. See the Chapter on Timing on page 227 for more information.

Hitting something also can occur after you have service your *Sewhandy* and either left something loose, or left a tool, i.e. small screwdriver, in the machine.

An extremely used machine can have bushings that are worn out and make a knocking sound as the internal parts rotate. This is a major repair. See the Chapter on Major Repairs on page 247.

28. Light inop, Light Switch inop:
Before you try anything else, make sure that there is power to the machine. Then try turning the light switch on and off a few times.

Light problems are usually the bulb. When buying a new bulb, get an exact replacement for your original. Two bulbs might look the same and have completely different voltage and current characteristics. Most bulbs are numbered and have the voltage on them. See the Chapter on Replacing Consumables on page 235 for the correct bulb.

Before installing the bulb, shine a flashlight into the bulb socket. See anything wrong? Sometimes the socket goes bad also. Look for green or white corrosion. If you find corrosion, it must be removed.

When installing the bulb, try not to cross thread it. If it does not thread in easily, there is something wrong. Remove it and inspect. Repair as necessary. Make sure the bulb is installed properly.

Maybe you have determined that the bulb and bulb socket are good... and it still does not light. How easy is it to get to the switch? You need to determine how much trouble it will be to test and replace. Ask yourself honestly, is this beyond my abilities? If so, drop the machine off at your Certified Sewing Machine Technician or email me at <u>Dar-Bet@att.net</u> .

Ok, you have decided that you have the ability. Before you start tearing things apart, read the theory and study the wiring diagram on page 97.

The simplest way to test a switch is with a multimeter. The power will always be OFF, and you will be checking for continuity. DO NOT PERFORM this test with your *Sewhandy* plugged in to AC Voltage. Remove the Power cable from the plug and the *Sewhandy*.

Perform continuity checks from the *Sewhandy* rear connector to the bulb socket center connector and to the outer threaded socket connector. Repair as necessary. Replacement Light Shade and Socket Assemblies are available. Email me at <u>Dar-Bet@att.net</u> .

29. Lightning strike: If you have a direct lightning strike, the *Sewhandy* motor and the Foot Pedal will probably be damaged beyond repair. Read the theory and check out the wiring diagram on pages 96 - 97. Replacement components are available. Email me at <u>Dar-Bet@att.net</u> .

30. Locked up with no movement : A hand wheel that is hard to turn or locked is usually the result of thread jams or a gearing problem in the machine. To determine if this is the problem, just take the belt off and try to turn the hand wheel. It should move easily, if not check the shuttle hook and feed dog drive path, and the needle drive path. See the Chapter on Mechanical Operation on page 81.

31. Loose stitches on bottom of fabric: See the Chapter on Tension on page 217.

32. Loose stitches on top of fabric:
See the Chapter on Tension on page 217.

33. Lower thread repeatedly breaks:
Make sure the bobbin is inserted in the bobbin case correctly and rotates (feeds) from the correct direction. Make sure the bobbin is evenly wound. Check the needle plate for damage.

34. Lubrication: See the Chapter on Lubrication on page 127.

35. Motor has no speed adjust: See Foot pedal does not vary speed.

36. Motor runs, but machine doesn't: The belt may be off the pulleys, or worn out or broken. The motor pulley setscrew may have come out letting the pulley spin on the motor shaft. The machine could also be locked up – See Locked up with no movement.

37. Motor smells like hot oil: This is usually caused by the use of oil in a grease type motor, i.e. the OSANN-SINGER. The smell can also be caused in a GE Motor if too much oil is used. The problem is caused by the excess oil being vaporized around the commutator. The fix requires cleaning the motor of the excess oil. Eventually, the excess oil will burn off and the

smell will lessen. See the Chapter on Lubrication on page 127.

38. Motor smokes: This could be a case of excess oil, or it could be a motor on its "last legs". Disconnect the electrical power from the *Sewhandy* and check the outside temperature of the motor by running your fingers over it.

It should be warm, but not hot. If it is too hot to touch, immediately discontinue using the *Sewhandy*. There is something seriously wrong with the motor.

See the Chapter on Motor Disassembly and Brush replacement on page 137 for more information. Email me at <u>Dar-Bet@att.net</u> for more information.

39. Motor throwing sparks: Motors using a commutator and carbon brushes always spark. However, no sparks should be evident outside the motor case. Excessive sparking may be caused by extreme wear of the commutator and/or carbon brushes. Repair may be possible by turning of the commutator and/or replacement of the brushes may fix the problem.

See the Chapter on Motor Disassembly and Brush replacement on page 137 for more information. Note: Other problems can also cause excessive sparking. Email me at <u>Dar-Bet@att.net</u> for more information.

40. Needle bar not moving up/down: Open the endplate up and watch the needle bar drive as you move the hand wheel. If you see rotation, follow the movement to the broken part. Repair as necessary. If there is no movement, remove the top arm cover (spool pin plate) so that you can see the miter gears.

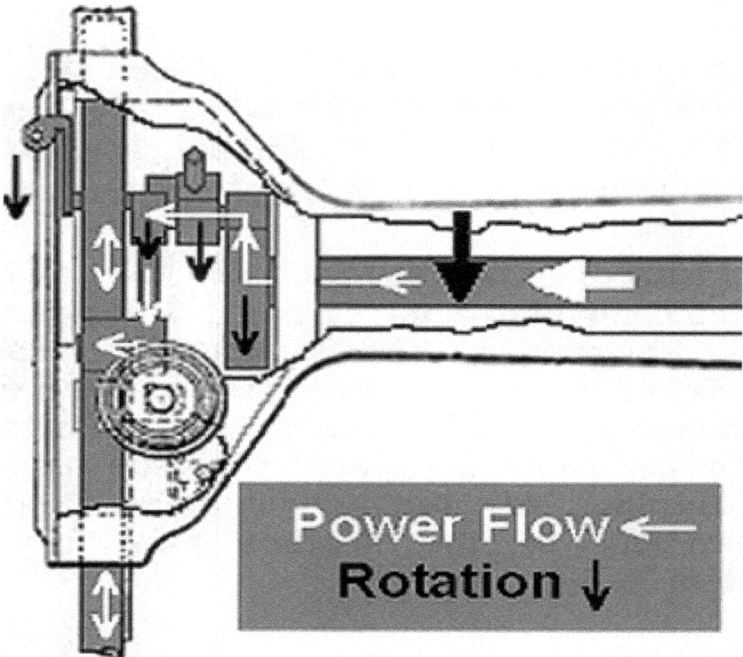

Power Flow ←
Rotation ↓

Check if there is any movement of the miter gears or Arm shafts as you turn the hand wheel.

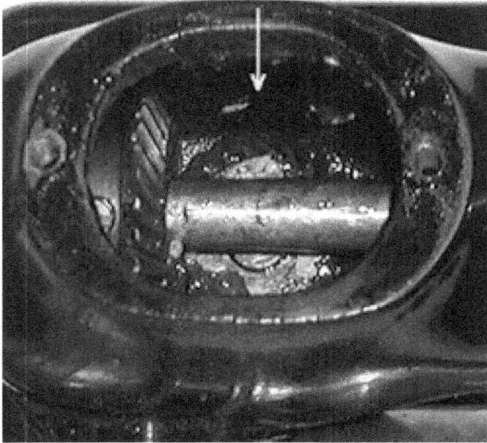

MITER GEARS

If there is no movement, the problem is with the bottom Arm Shaft (Vertical) Bevel gear or the Hook Shaft Bevel Gear. Read the Chapter on Mechanical Operation on page 81.

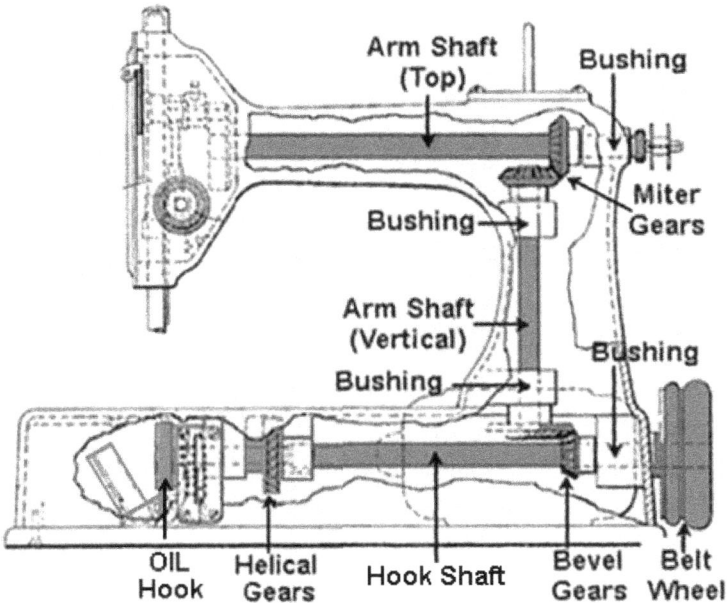

Arm Shaft (Top)

Bushing

Bushing

Miter Gears

Arm Shaft (Vertical)

Bushing

Bushing

OIL Hook

Helical Gears

Hook Shaft

Bevel Gears

Belt Wheel

41. Needle bent: Needles do bend without breaking. Extended embroidery sewing at high speed can actually warp a needle. See <u>Needles</u> and the Chapter on Timing on page 227.

42. Needle breaking: Needles can get so hot that they bend and break. However, if your needle keeps breaking then it is hitting something. Remove the power from your *Sewhandy* and watch and listen while you slowly rotate the hand wheel. You will be able to tell when it hits something. Usually, it is a problem with an incorrectly mounted needle. It may also be the needle plate or the *Sewhandy* timing. Repair as necessary. Read the Chapter on Mechanical Operation on page 81 for more information. See the Chapter on Timing on page 227 for more information.

43. Needle hits Pressor Foot: This is caused by one of five conditions: A) Needle bent, B) Pressor Foot bent, C) Pressor Foot Bar bent, D) Pressor Foot mounted crooked, or E) Pressor Foot loose. Repair as necessary.

44. Needle hits something below throat plate: Remove the power from your *Sewhandy* and watch and listen while you slowly rotate the hand wheel. You will be able to tell when it hits something. Usually, it is a problem with an incorrectly mounted needle.

The needle may be hitting the hook because the machine timing is wrong. Repair as necessary. Read the Chapter on Mechanical Operation on page 81 and see the Chapter on Timing on page 227 for more information.

It could also be that you have the wrong needle installed and that the needle is hitting the bobbin case (needle to long). I strongly recommend SCHMETZ 130/705H needles. Some other brands with similar numbers may be too long and may hit the bobbin case. This usually does not damage the bobbin case, but it will quickly dull the needle point. To check yours is a fairly simple process:
   1. Remove bobbin case from *Sewhandy*.

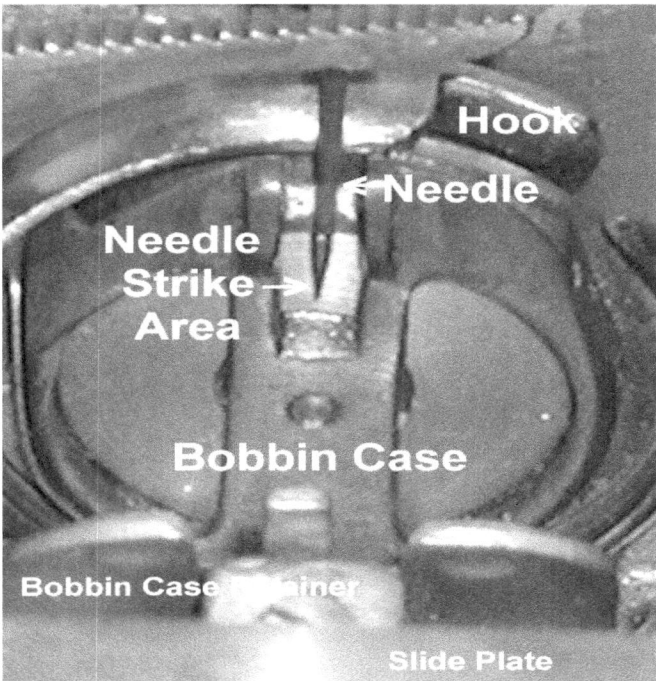

2. Use a light coat of white correction fluid, i.e. Wite-Out®, to paint the Needle Strike Area identified in the picture below. Let dry for 5 minutes.
3. Reinstall bobbin case in *Sewhandy*. Latch bobbin case retainer.
4. Slowly rotate hand wheel 3 or 4 complete turns.
5. Remove bobbin case from *Sewhandy*, and check for any needle strike marks in painted area. If you see some, your needle is too long (replace). If there are no marks, your needle is the correct length.
6. Remove correction paint from bobbin case and reinstall.

45. Needle hits throat plate: Needles do bend without breaking. Extended sewing at high speed can actually warp a needle enough that it will hit the throat plate. An incorrectly mounted needle can also cause this problem. Remember that the *Sewhandy* needle is mounted flat side to the right.

A loose needle bar with worn bushings can also cause this problem, but this condition should be readily apparent.

46. Needles: The condition of the needle is the most common problem that interferes with sewing. Bent or damaged needles will cause a variety of sewing problems. The way the needle

is inserted into the needle clamp is also extremely important.

With the *Sewhandy*, the 15x1 needle must be installed all the way to the top with the Flat side of the needle facing toward the <u>right side</u> of the *Sewhandy*. This is exactly opposite the **SINGER** Featherweight which faces the Flat to the left.

I strongly recommend **SCHMETZ 130/705H** needles. Some other brands may be too long and may hit the bobbin case (see Needle hits something below throat plate). There are a huge and confusing variety of needles to choose from these days, however some old rules to help us pick the right one still hold true. Use sharp points for woven fabrics, ball-point needles for knits and universal points for both woven and knits. Needle sizes are usually marked with European and American numbers, with the European number first. Needle sizes range from 60/8 (finest) to 120/19 (thickest).

Here is some generic needle information:
<u>Ball-point/stretch</u> needles have a rounded tip that pierces between the threads of a knit fabric.

<u>Sharp (Microtex)</u> needles have a sharp point to pierce the threads of woven fabric. They are good for heirloom sewing and quilt piecing.

<u>Universal needle</u> points are slightly rounded for use with knit fabrics, yet sharp enough for woven fabrics.

Denim/jeans needles have an extra-sharp point and stiff shank for stitching denim, heavy faux leather and other densely woven fabrics.

Leather needles have a wedge-shaped point to penetrate leather, suede, heavy faux leather and nonwoven fabrics.

Machine embroidery needles are designed to prevent thread shredding and breakage when sewing dense designs with rayon, metallic and other embroidery threads.

Metallic needles feature a long eye, fine shaft and sharp point to eliminate thread breakage, skipped and shredding stitches, and also work well with monofilament threads. They are sometimes called Metallica, Metafil and Metallic Machine Embroidery.

Quilting needles have a sharp tapered point to sew through thick layers and across seams.

Topstitch needles have an extra-sharp point, larger eye and groove to handle top-stitching thread.

47. Noisy: This can be cause by lack of lubrication, loose parts, or worn parts. Rotate your Sewhandy by hand and listen for where the noise is coming from. Check the gears for damaged teeth and correct mesh. See Knocking Sound and Hitting Something. Also see the

Chapters on Major Repairs (page 247) and Lubrication (page 127).

48. No light: See <u>Light inop, Light Switch inop</u>.

49. No movement: If the Belt/Hand Wheel will not rotate and the *Sewhandy* is mechanically locked up, see <u>Locked Up with no movement</u> and the Chapter on Mechanical Operation on page 81.

If the *Sewhandy* will manually rotate, but will not electrically operate with the Foot Pedal, see <u>Foot pedal inop (does nothing)</u> and the Chapter on Electrical Operation on page 95.

50. No power: See <u>Foot pedal inop (does nothing)</u>.

51. No speed adjustment: See <u>Foot pedal does not vary speed</u>.

52. No stitch length adjustment: The Stitch Length adjustment in the Sewhandy is completely mechanical. Mechanical controls are subject to corrosion and wear. If you cannot easily move a mechanical control, do not force it. You will damage it. The control may need replacement, or it may simply need cleaning or lubrication. If there is no lever movement, then the linkage is probably dry or corroded. If there

is lever movement, but no change in the Feed Dog movement, then linkage is disconnected or broken. See page 92 for more information.

53. Nothing moving: If the Belt/Hand Wheel will not rotate and the *Sewhandy* is mechanically locked up, see <u>Locked Up with no movement</u> and the Chapter on Mechanical Operation on page 81.

If the *Sewhandy* will manually rotate, but will not electrically operate with the Foot Pedal, see <u>Foot pedal inop (does nothing)</u> and the Chapter on Electrical Operation on page 95.

54. No upper drive movement: See <u>Needle bar not moving up/down</u>.

55. Operates by itself: See <u>Foot pedal not plugged in, yet machine runs</u>.

56. Poor Stitch Quality: This may be caused by the following:

a) The needle is incorrectly inserted. Check that the flat of the needle is inserted all the way to the top with the flat to the right.

b) The needle is blunt or bent. It should be changed before each large project, every 8 hours, or if it hits the needle plate or hook.

c) The tension is not correct. Make sure the

thread is between the tension discs. Make sure the Pressor Foot is up when you thread your *Sewhandy* (this will release the tension discs) Check for lint or thread caught between the discs. See the Chapter on Tension on page 217.

d) The type and make of the thread used can cause problems. Always use good quality thread. The thread must fit the needle.

57. Power surge: If you experience a power surge the *Sewhandy* motor and the Foot Pedal may be damaged beyond repair. Read the theory and check out the wiring diagram on page 97. Replacement components are available. Email me at <u>Dar-Bet@att.net</u> .

58. Presser Bar bent: This only occurs if the machine has been severely damaged somehow. Usually if the bar is bent, it will not move up and down to apply or release the downward pressure. Repair of this problem requires removal of the bar from the machine. Sometimes the bar can be straightened with a press. If not, I suggest replacement. Email me at <u>Dar-Bet@att.net</u>.

59. Presser Foot bent/crooked: This only occurs if the foot has been damaged somehow. What may be more likely is that the foot is not mating correctly on its mounting surface. Check for a tight fit with no play in the mounting. If the pressor foot is damaged, I

suggest repair or replacement. Email me at <u>Dar-Bet@att.net</u>.

60. Presser Foot loose:

If the rectangular groove in the *Sewhandy* Presser Foot has been damaged or somehow widened, then you may have a loose foot. The *Sewhandy* has a threaded nut that screws down and tightens on the Presser Foot flange. This system is maintenance free unless there is corrosion in the threads. You could also have problems with the Presser Foot Nut if someone removed it and then accidentally cross-threaded it on re-installation.

61. Presser Foot mounted crooked:

This can only be a defect in the mount. However, always make sure that the Pressor foot lines up with the feed dogs below. If it does not, then the fabric may not feed straight.

62. Runs intermittently: This may be
caused by a problem with the Foot Pedal front connector, the Foot Pedal itself, *Sewhandy* internal wiring, the Main Power rear connector, the motor, or the *Sewhandy* to 120VAC power cord. With everything plugged in correctly, try to turn the light on. If it lights (assuming the bulb is good), then you can eliminate some of the possible causes.

It is very important to remember that this is a non-polarized and an ungrounded system. The design of the interior of the Foot Pedal is such that the outer case is insulated from the *Hot* side. However, if the insulation were to be disturbed and fail, then there is a strong chance of electrical shock. Refer to pages 105 - 111 for Foot Pedal theory.

63. Runs slow: This can be caused by mechanical problems or electrical problems. Mechanical problems include Belt to tight (see <u>Hand wheel hard to turn</u>), lack of oil and lubrication (see <u>Lubrication</u>), and thread or fabric caught in moving parts (see <u>Thread Jamming</u>). Electrical problems include Foot Pedal (see <u>Foot pedal does not vary from half or slow speed</u>), and motor failures. See the Chapter on Electrical Operation on page 95.

64. Runs too fast: See <u>Foot pedal does not vary from full speed</u>.

65. Skips stitches: Check your upper threading, making sure the take-up lever is correctly threaded. Ensure that the needle is installed correctly (all the way to the top with the Flat side of the needle facing toward the <u>right side</u> of the *Sewhandy*). Inspect for needle damage and correct type of needle. Check your hook/needle timing. The needle and hook tip must meet at the correct time for the thread to be picked up. See the Chapter on Timing on page 227.

66. Stitch length Lever does not adjust stitch length – Stitch length Lever will not move: See <u>No stitch length adjustment</u>.

67. Stitch length varies: See <u>Feed Dogs not moving fabric</u>.

68. Stitching problems: See <u>Poor Stitch Quality</u>.

69. Switch inop: See <u>Light inop, Light Switch inop</u>.

70. Switch intermittent: See <u>Light inop, Light Switch inop</u>.

71. Take-up lever arm hitting case:
Occasionally, the Take-up Lever will get banged and slightly bent. This will cause it to rub on the *Sewhandy* frame or the Faceplate. The trick here is to adjust the lever back to its original position without damaging it or the linkage it is attached to. Refer to the drawing on page 87.

Remove the two screws that hold the Faceplate on. Remove the Faceplate and locate the Take-up lever. Using needle-nose pliers gently hold the lower part of the Take-up lever while you straighten the outside end of the lever so that it is back in its original position. Do not over bend. The key here is "Gently".

72. Tension discs: Check the tension discs to see if there is thread or lint stuck in the discs. This can cause low top tension and thread looping under the fabric. See the Chapter on Tension on page 217.

73. Tension loose on bottom:
See the Chapter on Tension on page 217.

74. Tension loose on top:
See the Chapter on Tension on page 217.

75. Tension will not adjust:
See the Chapter on Tension on page 217.

76. Tension wrong:
See the Chapter on Tension on page 217.

77. Thread balls: See <u>Balls under throat plate</u>.

78. Thread jams: Thread jams can occur anywhere on your *Sewhandy,* but the Take-up Lever, Feed Dogs, and Hook are usually the problem areas. Gently cut and remove the jammed thread. Do not pull and yank it out. Sometimes a little extra oil will help loosen the thread. Note: If you have been using "invisible" thread, it is very difficult to see and may require

the use of a flashlight. Invisible thread does not easily break and if wound a round a shaft can lock up any sewing machine.

79. Thread sheds or breaks: Thread that shreds or breaks is usually caused by a needle that is too small for the thread size. See <u>Needles</u>.

80. Timing wrong: See the Chapter on Timing on page 227.

81. Upper tension adjust inop: See the Chapter on Tension on page 217.

82. Upper tension intermittent: See the Chapter on Tension on page 217.

83. Upper tension wrong: See the Chapter on Tension on page 217.

84. Upper thread repeatedly breaks: Check the following: 1) that the needle is inserted correctly (all the way up and flat side to the right) and not damaged, 2) size of needle is correct for thread, 3) thread path (free movement of the thread from spool to needle), 4) ensure top tension is not too tight, 5) check the needle plate for damage, and 6) check the hook for damage. Adjust or repair as necessary.

85. Vibration: Vibration can be caused by many things. One bad bottom foot can cause an uneven platform. A loose part anywhere in the upper or lower drive train can also cause vibration. Worn out bushes or bearings, bad motor bearings, a bad belt, or a loose or incorrectly mounted hand wheel or belt wheel can also be the source (see <u>Hand Wheel problems, Hand Wheel Locked</u>).

The goal here is to eliminate each possibility one at a time starting with the most likely and the easiest to check.

Where would I start? I would check the bottom feet, then hand wheel, then the belt, and then the motor. Check the whole machine for loose parts.

Checking an operating sewing machine with the covers off and the all the mechanical parts rotating can be very dangerous. Unfortunately, there is no other way that I know of to find that elusive vibration. With this in mind, I recommend that you leave this to your experienced Sewing Machine Technician.

However, if you are determined to do this yourself, keep the machine speed as low as possible to find the vibration. Remember your safety equipment such as eye protection. Keep aware of all moving parts and remember that those rotating parts will grab any tool out of your hand and eat it (damaging the machine) or worse yet, then throw it back at you....

86. Will not feed: See <u>Feed Dogs not moving fabric</u>.

For help with other problems not listed in this chapter, email me at <u>Dar-Bet@att.net</u> with a complete description of the fault. Your description should be detailed and complete enough to answer the following questions at a minimum.

1. When does the problem happen?
2. What actually is wrong?
3. What actually happens?
4. How often does it happen?
5. What have you already done to fix it?
6. Visible symptoms or noise?
7. Make and model of your *Sewhandy*?

TENSION & YOUR
Sewhandy

The ability to correctly set the tension on any sewing machine is a skill that has to be learned over and over. Each machine type has its own unique adjustment. In fact, machines off the same production line will have slightly different tension levels and require slightly different adjustments.

What is tension? Tension is the amount of <u>extra drag</u> that we introduce into the threading so that the top and bottom loop formation will be balanced (or unbalanced for some decorative stitches).

Why do I call it extra drag? All machines have some friction or drag in the thread path. Put a spool on and thread the machine all the way to the needle with NO or Zero tension on the tension adjust. Give the thread a pull and you will feel some resistance. That is the built-in drag that all machines have. When you dial in more tension with the tension adjust, you are just adding extra drag.

I used the top tension thread in the example above. The bottom or bobbin case tension works just the same and also uses extra drag. In the bottom tension, there is a flat plate that is adjustable to vary the drag on the bobbin thread. You set the bottom tension using either a gram scale or a weight. Once set, the bottom tension is usually left alone.

Most tension adjustments are accomplished using the top thread tension adjustment assembly. Modern computerized machines adjust this automatically for each stitch type and feed speed.

The goal here is to sew the stitch that you want. Years ago, the idea was to have the top and bottom threads meet exactly in the middle of the fabric. The top and bottom tension were perfectly balanced. See the drawing below.

Needle - Top Thread

Bobbin- Bottom Thread

When I went thru Bernina University, I was taught that the current idea is to have the top and bottom threads meet at the bottom edge of the fabric. The top tension was less than the bottom tension. The idea was that the bottom bobbin thread would never show and spoil the sewing on the top side. This could be created by needle – top tension too loose or bobbin – bottom tension too tight. See drawing on the next page.

Needle - Top Thread

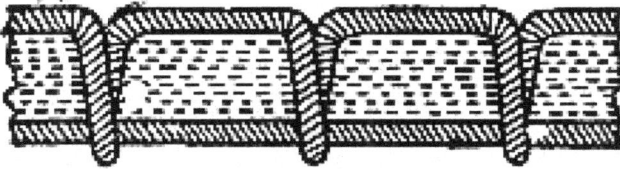

Bobbin- Bottom Thread

Some decorative stitches use the bottom stitch showing as part of the decoration. These require that the bottom tension is less than the top tension. This could be caused by needle – top tension too tight <u>or</u> bobbin – bottom tension too loose. See drawing below.

Needle - Top Thread

Bobbin- Bottom Thread

Think of the tension adjustment as a "dance." One only works WITH the other. If you raise the top tension, you are also lowering the bottom tension.... And if you lower the top tension, you are also raising the top tension.

If you pull the bobbin case, and adjust the screw to raise the bobbin tension, you are also actually lowering the top tension.

This is why the normal recommendation was to use the same thread in both top and bottom. Today, some will use a different thread in the bottom and wonder why the tension requires readjusting. Even changing to a different make of thread in either the top or bottom will change the tension relationship between the top and bottom. Remember to make only one tension adjustment at a time and check its effect.

I had a customer that purchased a huge amount of inexpensive thread in Mexico. It was almost impossible to get it to work in her machine. The thread had two filaments with almost no twist. When it passed between the top tension discs it would untwist and flatten out causing intermittent tension. I eventually modified the machine to use ONLY that thread with the warning that if she wanted to ever use "good" thread she would have to totally readjust the tension parameters.

So how do we specifically adjust the tension on the *Sewhandy*? The *Sewhandy* manual tells us to start with the bobbin bottom tension.

Bobbin Bottom Tension

The *Sewhandy* method uses the "drop test" with the weight of the bobbin and bobbin case as the measuring tool. Pull out about 6 inches of thread and hang the bobbin case and bobbin by the thread. If the case begins to move downward, then the bobbin case tension is too loose.

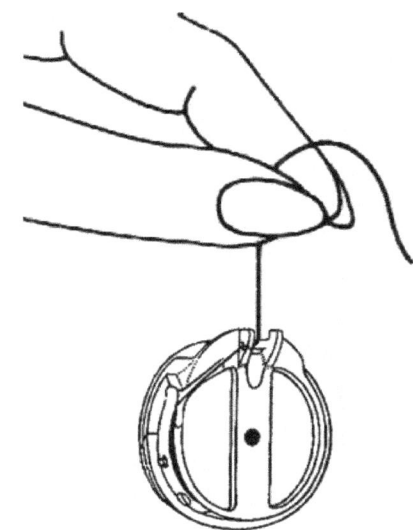

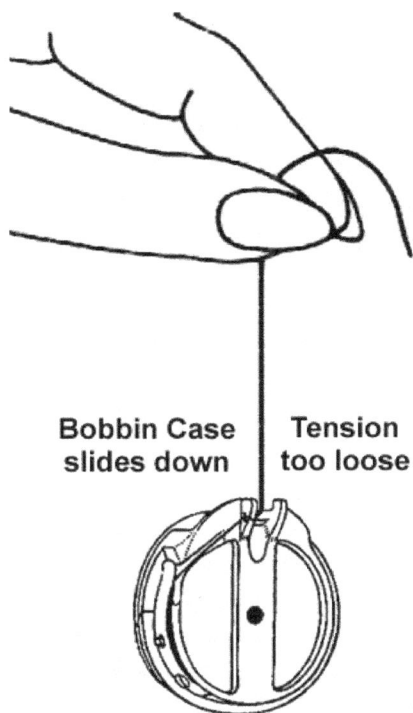

Bobbin Case | **Tension**
slides down | **too loose**

221

Use a small screwdriver and adjust screw "A" clockwise to tighten slightly.

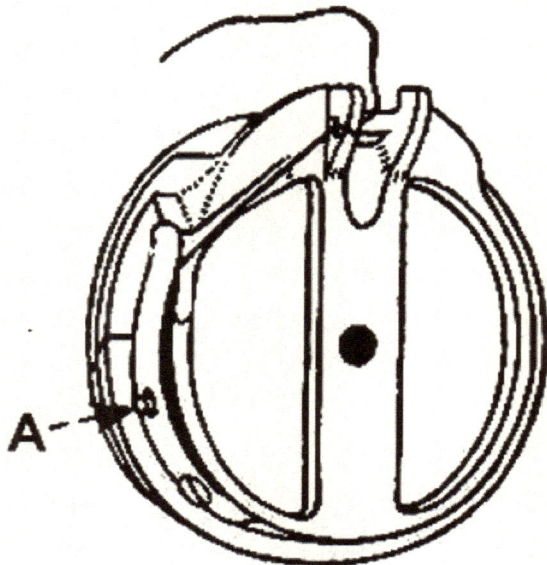

A--

Again, hang the bobbin case and bobbin by the thread. If the case still moves downward, then the bobbin case tension is still too loose. Continue to adjust screw "A" clockwise in small amounts to tighten and hang the bobbin case and bobbin by the thread until there is no downward movement.

The next step is to hang bobbin case and bobbin by the thread, but wiggle the thread slightly. The bobbin case and bobbin should <u>slowly move downward</u> as long as you are wiggling the thread. When you stop wiggling the thread, the bobbin case and bobbin should stop moving downward.

Thread Still - Bobbin Case Still

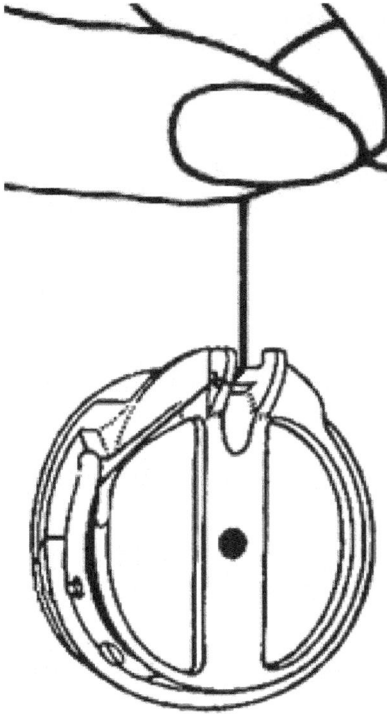

Thread Wiggled - Bobbin Slowly Slides Down

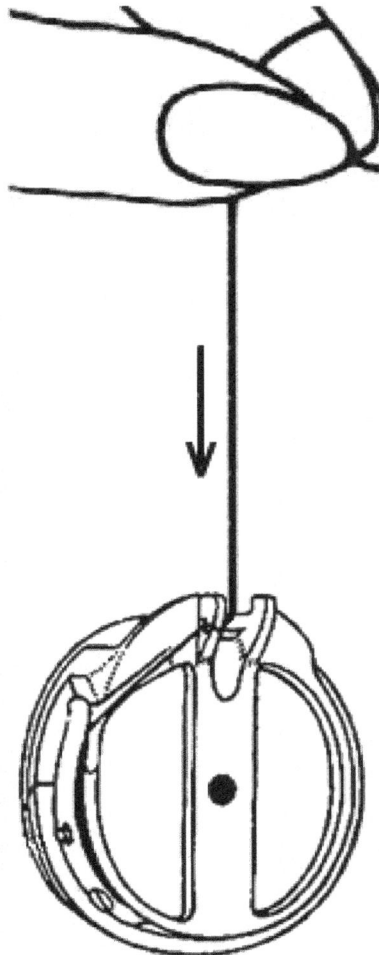

If it does both, the bobbin case tension is adjusted correctly.

If you have access to a bobbin case tension gauge (similar to below), the tension should work out to between 20 to 25 grams.

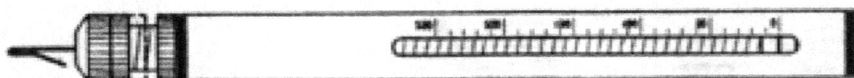

Put the bobbin case and bobbin back into the *Sewhandy* hook and latch the bobbin case retainer closed.

Needle Top Tension

The *Sewhandy* Needle Top tension is made-up of a regulating nut (C), a spring, and two tension discs. The tension discs provide more or less friction (drag) on the top thread as needed. The spring keeps the tension constant while the regulating nut provides the tension adjustment. Rotating the regulating nut clockwise will increase tension, while rotating it counter-clockwise will lessen the tension. The *Sewhandy* models do not have a reference dial.

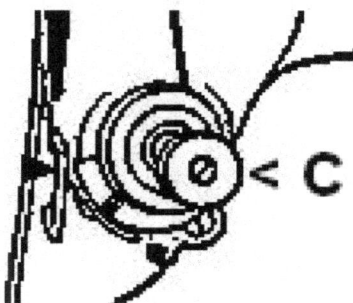

The method of adjusting the Needle Top Tension is one of trial and error. Sew on a piece of cloth and examine the stitch to see which one of the drawings below it most resembles. The goal is to be balanced like #3. Make the appropriate turns (small changes) to the Needle Top Tension regulating nut. Sew the stitch again to see which one of the drawings below it most resembles after your adjustment.

Always adjust the Needle Top Tension Top regulating nut FIRST. Do not adjust the Bobbin Bottom Tension unless you run out of adjustment using the Needle Top tension.

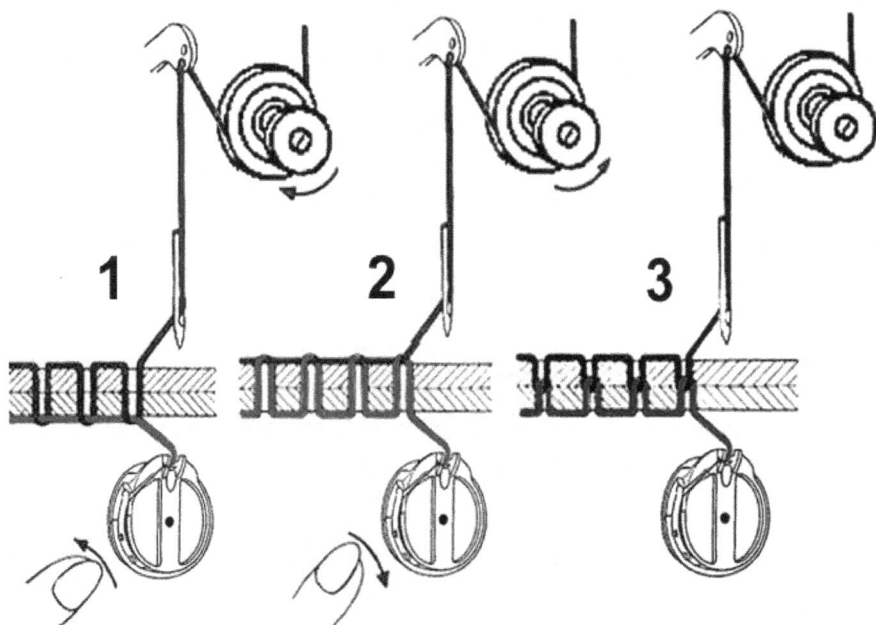

What Can Go Wrong?

The top tension is produced by the spring pushing against the tension discs to provide even drag on the thread.

If the spring or the discs are corroded or have other thread caught under them, the tension will be erratic. Check for both corrosion or thread. Clean as necessary.

Even small pitting of the disc surface can "catch' the thread and make the Needle Top Tension adjustment almost impossible. Polish with emery cloth as needed

A gummed up regulating nut will prevent full adjustment. Remove the nut and clean threaded stud as needed.

Last, if the thread is not actually <u>between the tension discs</u>, the tension will be incorrect. This happens more often than you would think on ALL machines.

Adjust the regulating nut as required. Make small adjustments. If you have access to a tension gauge (page 224), the tension should work out to between 20 to 25 grams.

226

TIMING YOUR
Sewhandy

No sewing machine will work unless it is correctly timed. Timing refers to the Needle drive movement, the Feed Dog movement, and the Hook rotation all happening at the correct time and sequence.

If it is all "in time," the machine sews. If it is out of time all sorts of problems can arise, i.e. broken needles, damaged bobbin cases and hooks, and jammed gears. Luckily, the *Sewhandy* is basically bullet-proof. The most likely damage is a broken needle.

Again, timing is the relationship between the Needle, the Feed Dogs, and the Hook. If your *Sewhandy* is sewing correctly, it is "in time." It might benefit from small adjustments even if the timing is good. Do not change the timing if your *Sewhandy* is already timed correctly or if you are not sure what you are doing. It can be difficult to correctly retime a machine.

To determine if your *Sewhandy* is in time, you need to observe the movement relationship of the Needle, the Feed Dogs, and the Hook.

Needle – Feed Dogs
First observe the Needle movement and the Feed Dogs movement. Turn the hand wheel clockwise (normal direction). Note the position

of the feed dogs as the point of the Needle reaches the top of the needle plate.

The Feed Dogs should be <u>down</u> below the needle plate surface, and just beginning to move forward. As the Needle continues down, stops, and then begins to move back up, the Feed Dogs have moved forward but are still below the needle plate surface.

As the Needle point is clearing the needle plate the Feed Dogs are rising above the needle plate to grab the fabric. The Needle continues to rise and while the Feed Dogs (at their maximum height) begin moving to the rear.

The critical point here is that the Feed Dogs <u>must not</u> be high enough to be able to move the fabric while the needle is still in the fabric or the needle will break. If the Feed Dogs do move the fabric while the Needle is still in the fabric, the timing relationship between the Needle drive and Feed Dogs is wrong. Note: Since the Feed Dogs and Hook are driven off the same shaft, both the Needle to Feed Dog timing and the Needle to Hook timing could be wrong at the same time. <u>Check both before adjusting anything.</u>

Needle – Hook

For the *Sewhandy* to sew, the Hook point must pass thru and catch the loop of thread formed by the Needle beginning its upward movement. This requires that the Hook rotate past the

Needle shaft slightly above the eye of the Needle as the needle is moving up. If the Hook does not catch the thread loop, the machine will not sew. Refer to the drawing below.

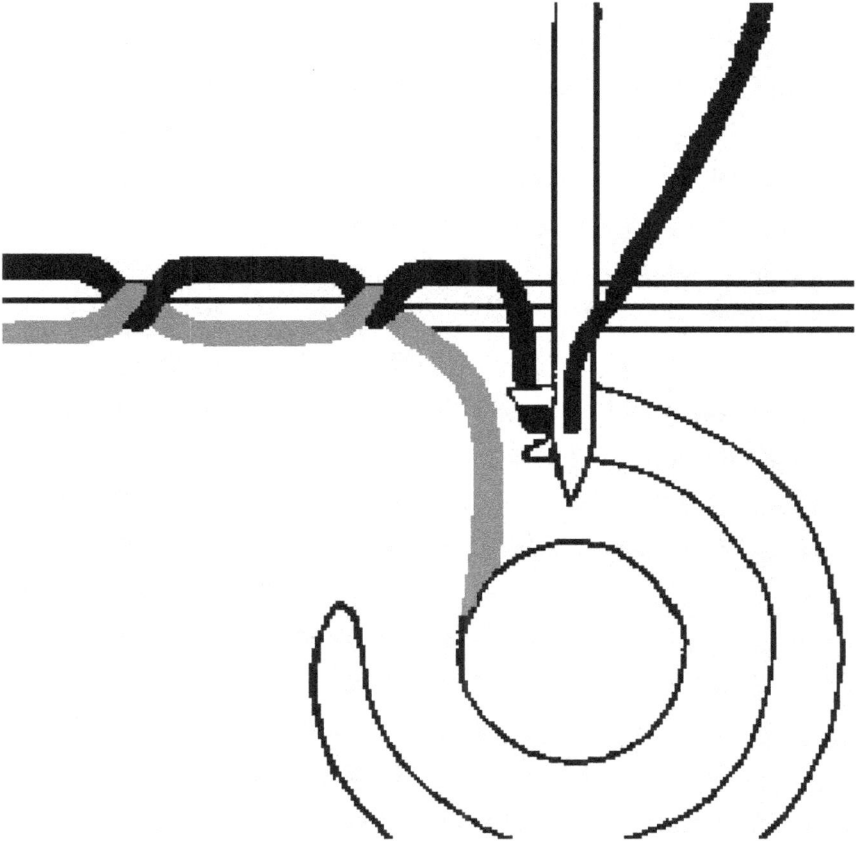

Refer to the picture of the *Sewhandy* Hook and Needle on the next page. Note that the Feed Dogs and Feed Dogs arm have been moved out of their normal position so that you can easily see the Needle to Hook relationship.

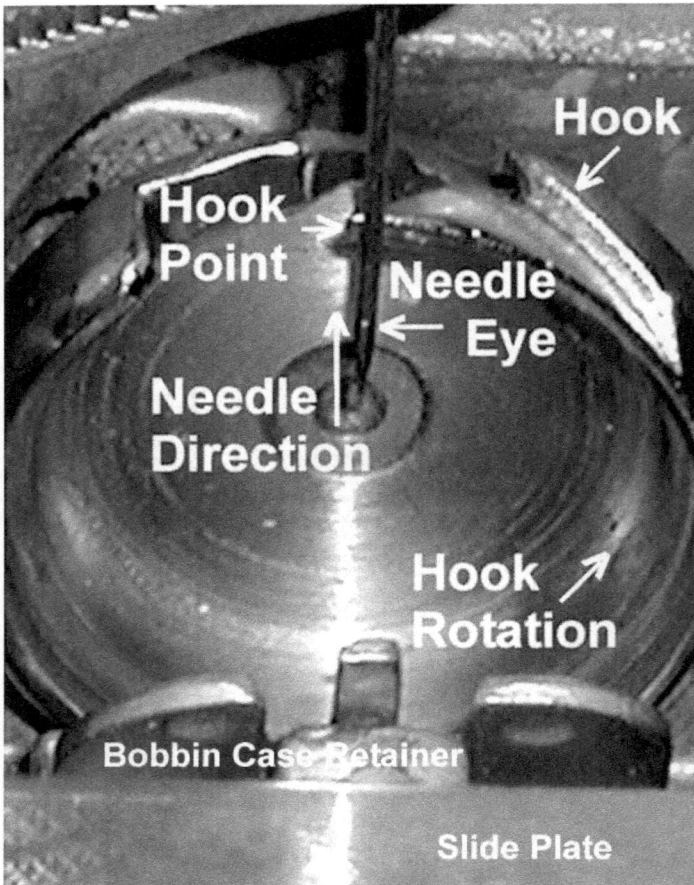

If the Hook passes the Needle <u>early</u>, the loop of thread will not have formed and their will be nothing for the Hook to catch. If the Hook passes the Needle <u>late</u>, i.e. after the Needle eye, then the loop of thread will be too high for the Hook to catch. The relationship of the Needle and Hook should be similar to that in the picture above; however, the *Sewhandy* will accept some latitude in the actual position.

From the previous paragraph on Needle to Feed Dog timing, we know that if the Needle is down then the Feed Dogs are also down below the throat plate surface. When the Hook is rotating past the Needle shaft slightly above the eye of the Needle as the Needle is moving up, the Feed Dogs are moving forward and slightly upward, but <u>are still below the throat plate surface</u>.

So how would the timing get messed up? On most sewing machines it happens because of a hard needle strike. This is especially true on modern machines with nylon gears or toothed belts. The shock of the needle hitting something causes the gear or belt to jump a few teeth. The result is a timing problem which causes more needle strikes and more jumped teeth.

The *Sewhandy* has brass gears so jumping teeth is not very likely. However, the needle strike could loosen the set screws holding the brass gears on to the shafts. The gears would be able

Gear Set Screws

to move on the shafts causing the timing to be off. The result is more needle strikes and more gear movement.

Timing Hints

1. If Needle to Hook timing is wrong, Needle to Feed Dog timing is wrong, and Feed Dog to Hook timing is correct:
   - Check the Arm Shaft Vertical and Arm Shaft Top Miter Gears for looseness.

MITER GEARS

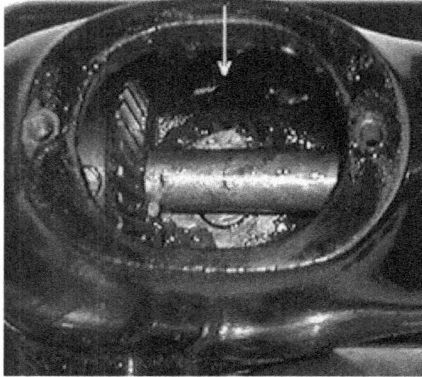

   - Check the Arm Shaft Vertical and Hook Shaft Bevel Gears for looseness.

BEVEL GEARS

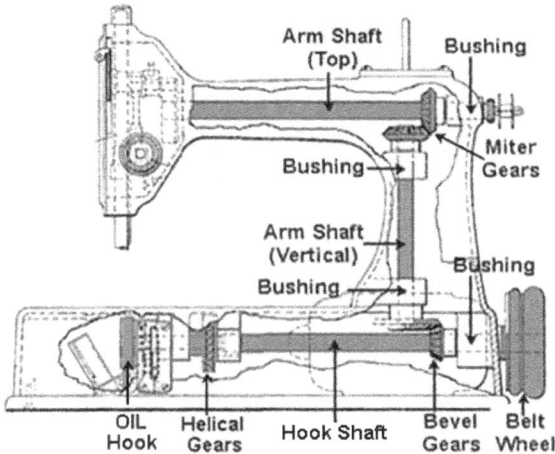

Arm Shaft (Top)
Bushing
Miter Gears
Bushing
Arm Shaft (Vertical)
Bushing
Bushing
OIL Hook
Helical Gears
Hook Shaft
Bevel Gears
Belt Wheel

2. If Needle to Hook timing is wrong, Feed Dog to Hook timing is wrong, and Needle to Feed Dog timing is correct: Check the Hook for looseness or movement.

3. If Needle to Feed Dog timing is wrong, Feed Dog to Hook timing and Needle to Hook timing is correct: Check the Hook Shaft Spur and Feed Shaft Helical Gears for looseness.

HELICAL GEARS

Adjustment

Adjust as necessary by moving the gears to meet the timing requirements explained on page 227. Note that the gears might have moved even if the set screws are still tight.

WARNINGS

Do not attempt to adjust the timing on your *Sewhandy* unless you completely understand the timing relationships. It is safer if you take it to a professional sewing machine technician.

The set screws on the gears must be tight in order for them to hold the gears in the correct position. If they are too loose, the gears will move out of correct timing. On the other hand, if you tighten them too much they will either strip the screw threads or gear threads. If you strip the screw threads, just replace the set screw. If you strip the gear threads, you can repair the gear with a thread insert. i.e. helicoil.

If you do decide to make adjustments, always do your initial sew-off test by rotating the belt wheel by hand. Do not use the electric motor until you are absolutely certain you have everything correctly timed.

REPLACING CONSUMABLES

The consumables that may need replacing are:
- Light Bulb
- Belt
- Machine Rubber Feet
- Needles
- Spool Spring and Felt
- Bobbin Case and Bobbin
- Sewing Machine Oil and Grease
- SINGER Machine Lubricant
- Motor Brushes
- Electrical cord
- Operating Manual

<u>Light Bulb</u> replacement: The bulb fits in to the General Electric Lamp Shade and socket. This socket is rated at a maximum of 75 watts @ 125V. A 120V bulb having a watt rating less than 75 watts with a 5/8-inch screw base (intermediate E17 base) will fit.

The higher the wattage the brighter the light; however, the higher the wattage the more heat that the light will emit. The usual bulb in the *Sewhandy* is a 10-watt 1-3/8 inch diameter bulb. Correct size bulbs are available, See Parts and contact author by email at Dar-Bet@att.net for availability and cost. Also visit:

www.SewhandySewingMachine.com

Belt Replacement: The drive belt is no longer commercially available. The belt is a round .230-inch cross section (CS) with about a 9.0 inch outside circumference. Note: Many sizes initially work; but belts that are too short WILL cause excessive wear on motor and belt wheel bushings. For a correct belt, see Parts and contact author by email at Dar-Bet@att.net for availability and cost. Also visit:

www.SewhandySewingMachine.com

Machine Rubber Feet: The original rubber feet are no longer available. However, functional substitutes are 5/8 to 3/4 inch polyurethane self-adhesive discs. Check your local hardware store, or see Parts and contact author by email at Dar-Bet@att.net for information. Also visit:

www.SewhandySewingMachine.com

Needles: There is some question whether a 1-7/16th versus 1-1/2 inch needle is correct for the *Sewhandy*. The correct needle is the standard 15x1. I strongly recommend SCHMETZ 130/705H needles. Some other brands may be too long and may hit the bobbin case (see Needle hits something below throat plate).

A picture of an original GE Needle package is below. It is important to use quality needles and to change the needle frequently. Remember that the Flat side of the needle faces the <u>right side</u> of the *Sewhandy* (Featherweight faces to the left).

Spool Spring and Felt: The spool felt and spring serve the same purpose on the *Sewhandy* as they do on the Featherweight 221. The felt protects the paint surface from damage caused by the high-speed rotation of the top thread spool.

The spring fits on the spool pin and keeps your spool from wobbling as it turns.

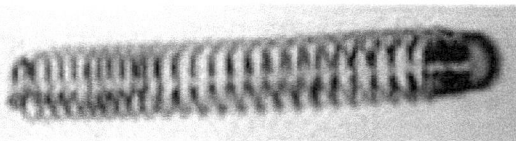

See Parts and contact author by email at <u>Dar-Bet@att.net</u> for availability and cost. Also visit: **<u>www.SewhandySewingMachine.com</u>**

Bobbin Case and Bobbin: The bobbin material is steel and its size is 0.83 inch outside diameter x 5/16th inch high with a 1/4th inch diameter hole. Original and replacement bobbins are also available from me.

The bobbin case has no current replacement. See Parts and contact author by email at <u>Dar-Bet@att.net</u> for availability and cost. Also visit **<u>www.SewhandySewingMachine.com</u>**

<u>Sewing Machine Oil and Grease</u>: Do not use any generic household oil, cooking oil, or automotive oil. Only use oil that is labeled as "sewing machine oil." Sewing machine oil is formulated for high-speed precision machinery, i.e. your *Sewhandy*. You can find a variety of brands at your local sewing center or fabric store. All sewing machine manufacturers promote their own brand of oil and if you have a favorite buy that one. I buy the generic type in a plastic bottle with an extendable spout

The *Sewhandy* manual recommends using Vaseline to lubricate the gears. Today, a better choice is white lithium grease. White lithium grease has lithium compounds that give the grease a better performance and temperature

range. It also adheres well to metal and resists flying off the gears from centrifugal force. With white lithium grease, you should only have to re-grease the *Sewhandy* gears every three or four years.

You can also buy this at your local sewing center or fabric store, but I find that it is cheaper (and just as good) at the local auto parts store.

NOTE: If you put oil where grease is supposed to be, any grease that was there will usually soften and just run out. What is left is a little oil, and a soon-to-be dry part.

<u>SINGER Machine Lubricant:</u> The OSANN SINGER motor does not use oil for lubricating. Do not use oil as it will eventually work its way to the brush assembly and compromise motor operation. SINGER specifies their Motor

Lubricant for this motor, just as it does for the Model 221 Featherweight motor.

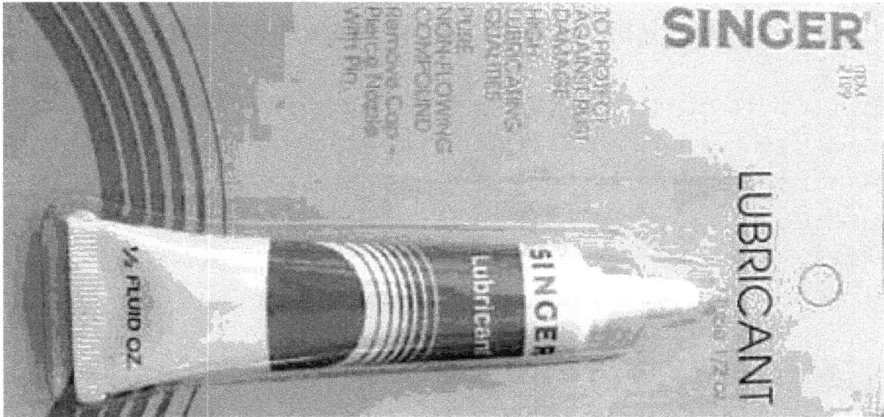

GE Motor Brushes: The two motor brushes are made of a longwearing carbon with spring assemblies. Each carbon brush is $5/32^{nd}$ inch square by $3/4^{th}$ inch long. Each spring is $1/8^{th}$ inch in diameter and has an uncompressed length of $3/4^{th}$. The brush and spring assemblies are similar to those used on the SINGER Model 221 Featherweight motor. However, they are not interchangeable as the Featherweight carbon brushes larger at $7/32^{nd}$ inch square with wider $13/64^{th}$ inch diameter springs.

Brush replacement, while extremely rare, will require removal of the Bottom Electrical Assembly and disassembly of the drive motor. While these tasks are not difficult, see the previous chapters on Electric Operation and Preventative Maintenance for instructions and hints before starting.

OSANN-SINGER Motor Brushes: Refer to the GE Motor Brush section above. While the motors are different, the GE and OSANN SINGER Motor carbon brushes are the same size.

Brush replacement, while extremely rare, will require removal of the Bottom Electrical Assembly. While this task is not difficult, see the previous chapters on Electric Operation and Preventative Maintenance for instructions and hints before starting.

Electrical Cord: The original Foot Pedal electrical cord was a two conductor AWG 20 stranded copper wire. Each individual conductor had a rubber insulator covering and a cloth wrap. Both wires were also covered as one with another black cloth covering. A modern replacement that looks very similar (but 18 gauge) is two conductor 18-gauge BLACK twisted COTTON wire (600V.105 deg C) available from:http://www.sundialwire.com .

The Bottom Electrical Assembly wiring also has one conductor AWG 20 stranded copper wires. As above, each wire had a rubber insulator and a cloth wrap. A modern replacement that looks very similar is catalog # W6ST-20BLK (20 gauge stranded 600v/105 deg C) available from: http://www.radiodaze.com .

Operating Manual: A copy of the Operating Manual is included in this book. For a separate reproduction copy of the Operating Manual, see

242

Parts and contact author by email at <u>Dar-Bet@att.net</u> for availability and cost. Please specify whether you want a SINGER-OSAAN *Sewhandy* or GENERAL ELECTRIC *MODEL A* manual. Also visit:

<u>www.SewhandySewingMachine.com</u>

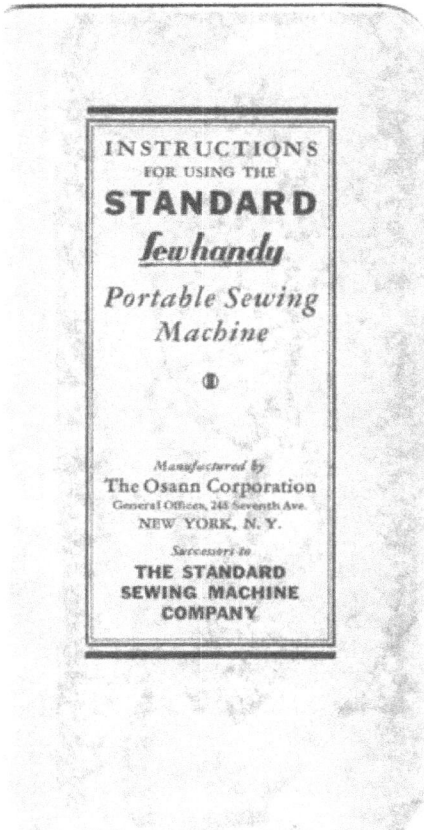

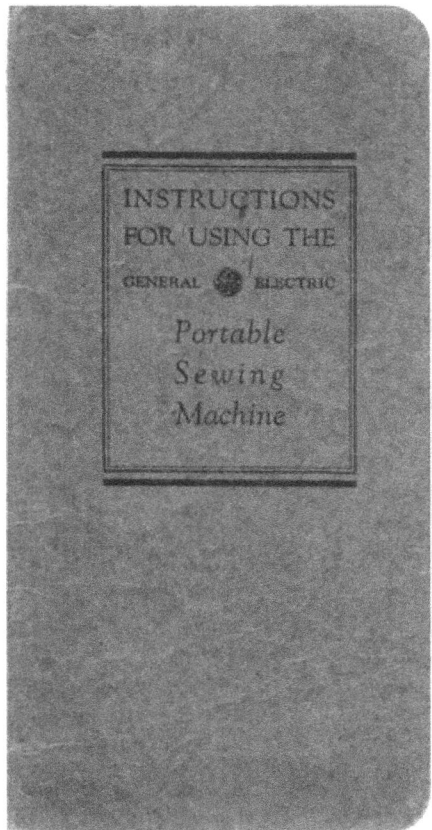

Copies of the SINGER B.U.K Electric Motor manual are also available.

Form K3691

INSTRUCTIONS

FOR USING AND ADJUSTING

SINGER

B.U.K. ELECTRIC MOTORS

WITH FOOT CONTROLLER FOR
FAMILY SEWING MACHINES

When requiring
Needles, Oil,
Parts or Repairs
for your Machine

Look for the
Red "S"
There are Singer
Shops in every City

THE SINGER MANUFACTURING CO.

1931

Original Manual Cover

244

Sewhandy PARTS

Consumables and many replacement parts are still available for your *Sewhandy*. These are divided into three categories:
1. New "Old Stock"
2. Reproduction or Generic
3. Refurbished Used

New "Old Stock"

Very little New "Old Stock" is available. Most of what is left is in a deteriorated state. It is also very expensive. Email me at <u>Dar-Bet@att.net</u> for more info or specific requests.

Reproduction or Generic

These are parts that are NEW and have been recently produced for, or modified for, use in the *Sewhandy.*

Refurbished Used

These are parts that have been removed from *Sewhandy* machines that are beyond repair. All of these parts are inspected and refurbished to meet *Sewhandy* requirements. They all carry a "Parts Replacement" warranty (covers replacement of part; does not cover shipping, and does not cover labor to replace part unless part was installed by author). Email me at <u>Dar-Bet@att.net</u> for more info or specific requests, or visit:

<u>www.SewhandySewingMachine.com</u>

Consumables & Parts List

- **Belt**
- **Light Bulb**
- **Bobbins**
- **Operating Manual (Reproduction)**
- **Singer BUK Manual (Reproduction)**
- **Spool Spring**
- **Spool Felt**
- **Rubber Bed Feet (4)**
- **Plus More......**

- **Refurbished Used – I stock most of the parts for the *Sewhandy* and *MODEL A*. Email me at <u>Dar-Bet@att.net</u> for more info or specific requests. These parts all require that you send in your original part or "core" to me. I refurbish the "cores" to save both of us money. If the original part is not available to turn-in, then I will charge an additional core charge.**

Some parts may be repairable, and I will repair your specific part (or *Sewhandy*). Email me at Dar-Bet@att.net for more info or specific requests, or visit:

<u>www.SewhandySewingMachine.com</u>

MAJOR REPAIRS

Major repairs to a *Sewhandy* are rarely needed. This chapter will only be important if you "accidentally" purchase a non-working machine, or if your *Sewhandy* suffers a catastrophe.

Major repairs include gear, bushing, and shaft removal. The hardest problem in any extensive repair is keeping track of what goes where when you reassemble. I suggest you take many digital pictures as you take your *Sewhandy* apart.

These instructions are not a recommendation that you perform them, but are here as educational information.

Part of this procedure involves the resetting of gear mating clearances and backlash, and sewing machine timing. Incorrect backlash and mating clearances, and timing WILL damage or destroy your *Sewhandy*. (Contact the author by email at <u>Dar-Bet@att.net</u> for prices on his service).

For access to the specific part, the following general steps would be accomplished (follow to the appropriate level):

Disassembly
1. Remove ALL POWER from sewing machine.
2. Disconnect all electrical cords; remove belt.

247

3. Unscrew the two screws holding on the Lamp Shade and Socket Assembly. Gently lay it aside. (It will still be hooked to the electrical cable). See picture below.

Remove ←

4. Remove two screws holding Spool Pin and Plate. Remove Spool Pin and Plate.

Remove

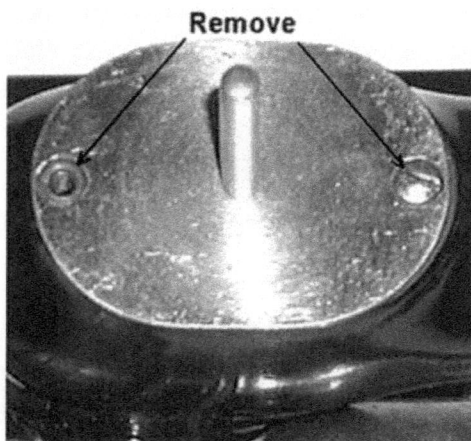

5. Gently turn machine over so that you are looking at the wooden bottom.

6. Only remove the FIVE screws that I have indicated in following the picture. Do not remove any the other screws now.

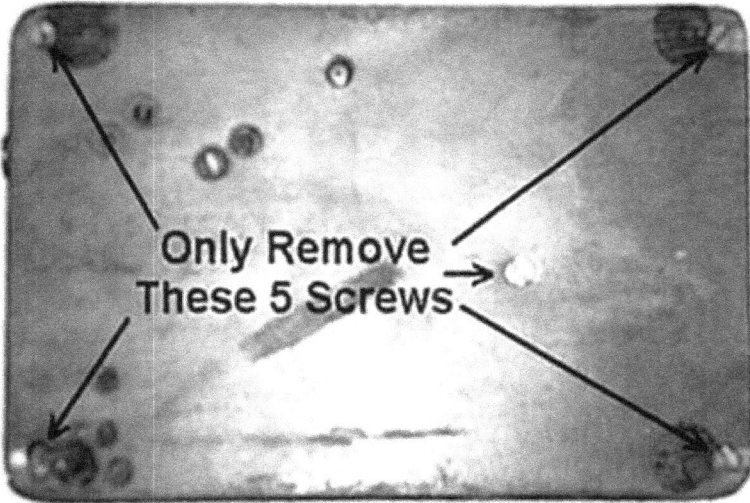

Only Remove
These 5 Screws →

7. While holding the neck of the machine in one hand and supporting the wooden base with the other hand, slowly lift the two assemblies apart.

8. Let the non-motor end of the wooden base tilt farther down. This will let the motor pulley slide though the machine hole.

9. Carefully guide the Lamp Assembly with its cable thru the top motor hole.

10. You now have two separate parts: The *Sewhandy* Mechanical assembly, and the Bottom Electrical assembly. Set the Mechanical assembly safely aside.

11. Disassembly of the Bottom Electrical Assembly (the GE or SINGER-OSANN motors) is covered in a previous section beginning on Page 243.

12. Disassembly of the Mechanical Bed Assembly continues- Remove as many of the covers as practical: the Slide plate, Needle plate, Face Plate, and Top Arm Cover. The goal is to expose as much of the inside of the *Sewhandy* as possible. I suggest that you use a magnetic holder to keep all the screws together in one place.

13. There are two sub-assemblies that make up the Mechanical Bed Assembly: the Bed Subassembly, and the Arm Subassembly.

14. Remove the Arm Subassembly by removing the three screws attaching it to the Bed Subassembly. You may have to use a razor blade to cut the paint on the exterior where the two subassemblies attach.

250

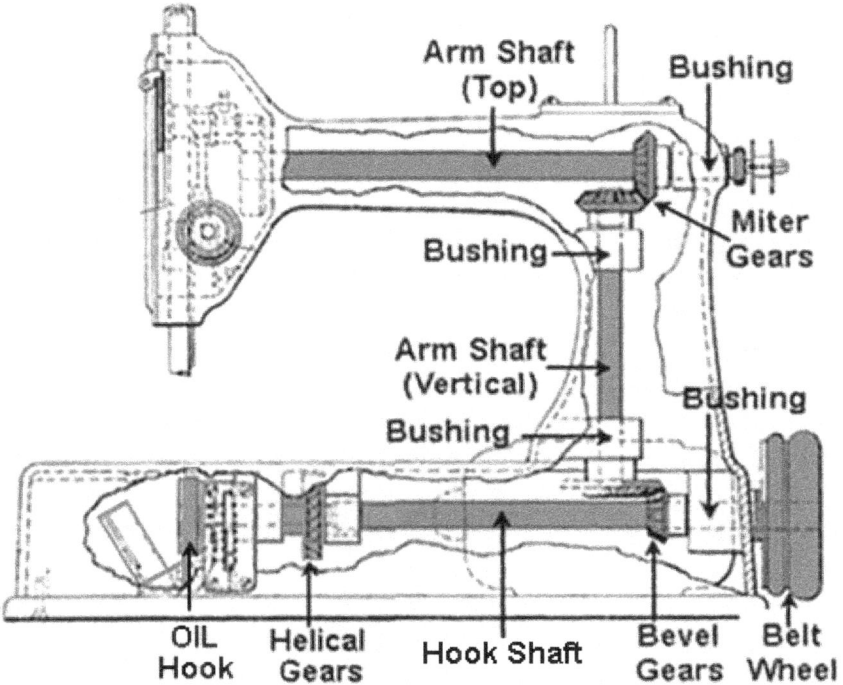

Arm Shaft (Top)

Bushing

Miter Gears

Bushing

Arm Shaft (Vertical)

Bushing

Bushing

OIL Hook   Helical Gears   Hook Shaft   Bevel Gears   Belt Wheel

15. **Further disassembly requires the removal of the set screw(s) holding the gears and bushings in their current positions. The photos on the next page show typical the gear set screws and bushing support set screws. For access to the Arm set screw, you will need to use the access holes already in the arm (they look like oil holes but are actually access holes). Note: Once you loosen a gear, the machine timing will be off and MUST be reset. Failure to correctly rest the *Sewhandy* timing will cause damage when you attempt to use it.**

251

The most common damage is that the needle will shatter when it tries to pierce the hook.

BEVEL GEARS

MITER GEARS

HELICAL GEARS

Cleaning

1. Remove all old grease or contaminants from the gears, bushings and shafts. Do not use anything abrasive on any of the parts. If need be, soak the components in a degreaser overnight. Make sure that you follow **ALL SAFETY** procedures when using any degreaser or petroleum products.
2. Use a soft brush to remove any remaining grease and wipe the part dry with a lint free towel.

Inspection

1. The goal is to find any defect in the *Sewhandy* parts.

2. Examine the shafts for wear. Compare the shaft diameter where it is in a bushing to where it is not in a bushing. If you have a micrometer or digital calipers take a measurement. Do this on more than one side as shafts can develop flat spots.
3. Lay the shaft on a flat surface and slowly roll it. This will check whether it is still straight or is bent.
4. Check the shaft flats for damage from the gear set screws. Some indentation is OK as long as the setscrew will correctly lock when you next install it.
5. Check each gear for broken or worn teeth. Gears occasionally crack so check for that. Check the inner diameter of the gear in relation to its shaft. Slide it on the shaft. It should be snug (not tight) with no wobble.

Left-Hand (top) and Right-Hand (bottom) Helical Gears meshing.

6. The gear teeth should not have a knife-edge; if they do they are excessively worn and should be replaced.
7. Check for corrosion on everything. Remove if possible WITHOUT damaging the part. If you cannot remove the corrosion, there are commercial products that will stop and seal the corrosion.
8. Check each bushing inner diameter in relation to its shaft. Slide it on the shaft. It should be snug (not tight) with no wobble.
9. Look at everything for any signs of damage or defect such as cracks, needle strikes, over tightening, etc.

Repair or Replacement

1. Few of the *Sewhandy* parts are still available. However, an experienced machinist can still manufacture almost all the *Sewhandy* parts. Some parts like bent shafts can be straightened, and worn parts can have metal added to their surfaces. It only depends on how much money you want to spend on your *Sewhandy*.
2. Another source of parts is to purchase a second *Sewhandy* that has a horrible exterior condition.

Reassembly

1. This is when those pictures you took during disassembly become important. You did take pictures, right!

2. Reassembly is just the reverse of disassembly. Follow the previous steps in reverse.
3. Do not over tighten set screws. They will strip out the threads. If you do strip out the threads, there are thread inserts (i.e. helicoil) that you can install. Visit your local auto parts store for these.
4. While assembling the parts, lightly coat all surfaces with sewing machine oil.
5. You will be temporarily setting the gears, do not over tighten setscrews. The gears should mount on the same shaft flats as before. The gear teeth should mate with the other gear but not be tight with the other gear. At the same time, there should not be any backlash or play between the two gears teeth.
6. As you reassemble, rotate the shafts and gears to make sure nothing is binding. If you notice a drag, now is the time to fix the problem. Do not wait until you are finished assembling.
7. Assuming you have everything back in its proper place, rotate the belt wheel by hand and watch for any interference or rub. If you cannot get everything back in its correct place, email me for help.

Adjustment

1. All sewing machines are precisely adjusted, and their timing is critical. The relationship between the Needle Drive (Arm) and the Hook and Feed Drives (Bed)

must be correct and stay constant at any speed or load. If they don't, bad things happen. See Timing on page 227.

2. In addition to timing, you must ensure that the gears correctly mate with their partner, and that the setscrews holding them in the correct position do not loosen. It is very frustrating to go thru all the timing measurements, and then have a gear slip. Even so, do not over tighten setscrews. You may find it helpful if you use a liquid thread locker (i.e. Loctite 222) to keep the setscrews in. Use only the "removable" small screw type, not the "permanent" type.

3. Perform a complete lubrication of the *Sewhandy*. See the previous chapter on Lubrication for more info. Do not run the machine dry!

Test

1. Once you have everything reassembled and correctly timed, you can move on to testing. (Do not test until you are sure that the *Sewhandy* is correctly timed).

2. Plug Foot pedal power cord into front 2-prong female connector.

3. Plug Main Power cord into rear input 2-prong mail connector.

4. Plug Main Power cord in to 120VAC power strip.

5. Slowly press down on Foot pedal and power the drive motor. Run motor slowly for a few minutes.

6. Watch for and listen for anything unusual, i.e. smoke, noise, etc. Immediately disconnect power if you suspect a problem. If there is a problem I recommend that you take to your Sewing Machine Technician or email me.
7. Sew a sample, and evaluate the top and bottom stitch formation. Make final tension adjustments to the tension assembly and the bobbin case spring.

SALVAGING A
Sewhandy

Salvaging a *Sewhandy* is not the same as repairing a *Sewhandy* that has seen better days. Salvaging a flooded machine requires extensive maintenance and is best left to a professional sewing machine technician.

The majority of the damage to flooded machines is from rust. This even happens on machines that were not submerged, but only exposed for periods to the extreme dampness.

The highly polished shafts and rotating parts will quickly rust. Tension discs can be ruined in a matter of hours. Any *Sewhandy* exposed to these conditions should be serviced by your professional sewing machine technician as soon as is possible (sooner the better).

If professional servicing is not available, I recommend the following steps to temporarily minimize (not eliminate) further damage:

1. Allow the sewing machine to dry naturally in a warm, dry place.

2. Spray WD-40 or similar lightly on the metal parts to slow rusting. Do not let WD-40 get on plastic or rubber parts, or any electrical components.

3. After your *Sewhandy* is completely dry of water or moisture and at normal room temperature, seal the machine in a plastic bag and remove it from exposure to the weather and temperature changes.

Take it to your professional sewing machine technician, or ship it to me for repair as soon as you can.

Be sure to tell whoever services your *Sewhandy* that it was exposed to water. The technician will perform specific inspections and steps to eliminate any remaining moisture and minimize any corrosion wear or damage.

TO RESTORE or NOT RESTORE

To restore, or not to restore.... that is the question.

The chapter is concerned with exterior restoration, not mechanical restoration (see previous chapters for mechanical service).

Opinions pretty well split into two groups when restoration comes up. This is true for collectable furniture, collectable cars, and probably anything else collectable.

One group strongly believes that no restoration should be performed, and that the scratches and dings that the *Sewhandy* has only add to the value of the machine. The other group would like the *Sewhandy* restored so that it looks just like the day it left the factory.

The first group feels that any restoration devalues any vintage or antique sewing machine, while the second group feels it is a waste to not help an ailing machine and bring it back to its original beauty.

I think both groups will agree on two things:
1. A poor quality restoration is <u>worse</u> than no restoration at all. It also drastically reduces the value.

261

2. An outstanding restoration back to factory new is beautiful. While it will not raise the value to that of an un-restored perfect item, it will considerably raise the value over an un-restored junker.

Restoration Hints

Paint: The *Sewhandy* came in a variety of colors:

- (STANDARD) Green, Blue, Rose, and Black
- (FREDERICK OSANN) Larch Green, Marine Blue, French Maroon, Velvet Black
- (GE) Green
- (OSANN-SINGER) Black

While some of the colors may sound the same, each of the manufacturers had a slightly different color, i.e. STANDARD "Green" is not the same as FREDERICK OSANN "Larch Green". The one constant is that "Black" does seem always to be the same "Black".

Also, all paints tend to change slightly over years of exposure to sunlight and oils. Some colors show this more than others do.

In order to match the color and aged tint of your *Sewhandy*, I recommend that you take it to an automotive paint store and have the paint matched.

Completely repainting a *Sewhandy* is best left to a professional painter. Before painting, the *Sewhandy* will have to be disassembled so that none of the moving parts are painted.

I recommend repainting only the scratches and chips. Langka.com has a unique process that you may be able to use on your *Sewhandy*. I have used it with excellent results on a number of machines (website at http://www.langka.com).

Decals: Another problem with completely repainting the *Sewhandy* is the decal issue. There is no one making the individual decals for the different versions of the *Sewhandy* and *MODEL A*.

It is possible to make custom water slide decals using a computer and computer printer. Check the internet for suppliers. Remember, that the decals will have to be covered with some type of clear-coat or protective finish.

Chrome: Do not use any type of abrasive cloth or paper on shiny surfaces. Use a non-abrasive cleaner and a soft cloth only.

BUYING A *Sewhandy*

First, you need to decide why you want or what you want to do with the *Sewhandy* once you get it. Decide before you buy the machine.

If you are a collector and only want to show it off on a shelf as a mechanical object of art, then you will be more concerned with the 'look" and condition of the machine exterior.

Most *Sewhandy* machines have seen better days. I believe that this is because they have actually been used during their life.

Contrast this with a perfect Featherweight machine that is 60 years old with Zero scratches or pin strikes. Even the most careful sewers cause wear to their machines.

If you intend on using your *Sewhandy* for actual sewing, that is great. The *Sewhandy* sews just as well as the Featherweight, and is actually more stable.

Like all older machines, it does require maintenance. The more you often you use it, the more often you will have to maintain it.

One warning- Using the *Sewhandy* once a year is one of the worst things you can do.... You figure that you are not using it enough to require maintenance so you do not do it.... And the machine corrodes and gums up.

Condition Code

Many years ago, someone came up with a condition code that rated sewing machines numerically. When looking for a *Sewhandy*, you may see this code or some derivative of it. Higher is better; lower is worse.

10. The *Sewhandy* is just like the day it left the factory with no scratches or marks.

9. Close to 10, but can have the small odd scratch or wear mark visible only with close inspection.

8. Very good used. All paint is good with all metalwork bright. Average antique dealer would consider "perfect."

7. Good, but rubbing of paint visible with some metal plating worn.

6. Close to 7, but more wear to paint with some surface rust on metal.

5. Average hard-used *Sewhandy*...

4. Chipped paint and rusty metalwork.

3. Needs substantial restoration.

2. Total restoration needed to paint and bright metal.

1. Good for spare parts only, and those would require extensive restoration.

The Sewing Machine Center Or The Thrift Shop

Buying a *Sewhandy* from a sewing machine center is the ideal way to purchase one. The sewing machine technician will be able to tell you about it and give you some type of warranty.

The problem with buying from a sewing machine center is that few of them carry the *Sewhandy*. Usually, you will find one on a shelf in an out-of-the-way thrift or antique shop, and they will know no nothing about the machine or its condition.

eBay Auctions

eBay presents a whole different set of concerns. The site has everything from doorstops to museum pieces for auction. It is up to you to tell which is which.

You will be able to see the *Sewhandy*, but the picture will probably show the best view, not the worst. Read the text description carefully to make sure that you know what you are getting.

Some things to look for:
- Can you tell if the *Sewhandy* is properly threaded?
- Is a sample of the stitches shown?
- Is the light shown? Is it lit?

- Do you see a foot pedal, and is it plugged in?
- Does the Seller know how to operate the *Sewhandy*?
- If the Seller states something like: "I do not know how to sew, but the needle goes up and down when I turn the hand wheel," that only means that the needle does go up and down. It does not necessarily mean that the needle is in time with the feed dogs or even that *Sewhandy* will operate.
- Ask if it has been plugged in, and turned on. This may help you find out the condition of the motor.
- Verify that there is a bobbin case included, preferably with a threaded bobbin inside it.
- Look closely at the paint finish and decals. Check for adhesive tape on the bed that was used as a seam guide. Masking tape is nearly impossible to remove without damaging the paint.
- Many *Sewhandy* machines are shown with a makeshift pin cushion or pin collar attached to the upper arm. While this was convenient for the former owner, it usually leaves lots of small pin scratches and a damaged *Sewhandy* decal.
- What about the carrying case, and how does it smell? What about mildew and musty odors.
- Is there a *Sewhandy* operating book included?

Read all you can about the *Sewhandy* before you bid. The more you know the better bidder you will be. Compare what the seller says about the *Sewhandy* with what you learned in this book. Most sellers know very little about these models.

Find out everything you can about the Seller before you bid. Look at the Seller's feedback. Some questions to think about are:
- Have they sold machines before?
- Do they know how to pack one carefully?
- If not, will they honor your polite request to double-box the machine and pack/ship it as you request?
- One thing I would recommend is to absolutely, positively agree on how a machine will be packed and how it will be shipped BEFORE bidding.

Read and re-read the description until it is perfectly clear what they are selling, and what is not selling. Download the images and closely examine with an image program. Some questions to consider are:
- Is the listing a detailed one with lots of photos, or is the machine a dim blur?
- Can you see if there is a tension spring, or a bobbin case, or missing parts?
- Watch out for listings for electric machines that do not mention or show a foot pedal/control.

If in doubt, ask questions. If unsatisfied with the seller response, move on to another auction. Ask all your questions before you bid. i.e.:

- Where did the *Sewhandy* come from?

Make sure you and the Seller agree on everything before you bid. If you cannot agree before the sale, there is absolutely no chance you will agree after the sale.

There are *Sewhandy* sewing machines that should not be purchased unless you are buying for spare parts.

- Ones with corrosion or rust. This is a big "Red Flag" waving at you. If the exterior is corroded, then the bushings, shafts, and gears are also corroded. I call machines in this condition "Door Stops."
- Ones with the wrong motor voltages for your area, i.e. some GE *MODEL A*'s made for overseas were equipped with 220VAC motors. Retrofitting is possible, but it is never cheap.
- Ones with badly damaged paint. The seller will tell you that the damage adds to the "character' of the *Sewhandy*. Will it still add to the "character" after you have owned it for a few months? The paint is available, but the decals will have to be specially created by someone. It can be done, as I have explained in the restoration section... but it is not easy.

- Machines with missing parts. You see these all the time, "Works great, but foot pedal is missing" or "Sews good, but bobbin case is missing." Ask yourself how did they power it up without a foot pedal, or sew without a bobbin case? Hooks are often missing, as are the Bobbin Retainers. Parts are scarce and it is better paying a little more for one has everything.

- Machines that will not rotate by hand. This could be caused by old gummed-up oil and grease, or it could be more serious and have seized. Parts are scarce and it is better paying a little more for one that works.

Of course, everything does depend on price. If you get one really cheap, have a professional sewing machine technician give it a once over. The machines are no more difficult than a Featherweight. They are much simpler to repair than a 1970 Singer... If you want an opinion on one, email me. If you need one repaired, email me at <u>Dar-Bet@att.net</u> for a price or visit:

www.SewhandySewingMachine.com

SHIPPING YOUR
Sewhandy

One of the worst mistakes that people make in shipping the *Sewhandy* machine is thinking that the carrying case will protect it during shipment. The machine will be protected from any outside dangers, but it will destroy itself, or the case, by banging around inside the case. (This is the same problem with Featherweights).

I have seen *Sewhandy* machines break the bottom of their case completely out during rough shipping.

The Sewhandy case does have a wooden machine retainer cleat at the bottom. Do not depend on the cleat to hold your *Sewhandy* down in rough shipping.

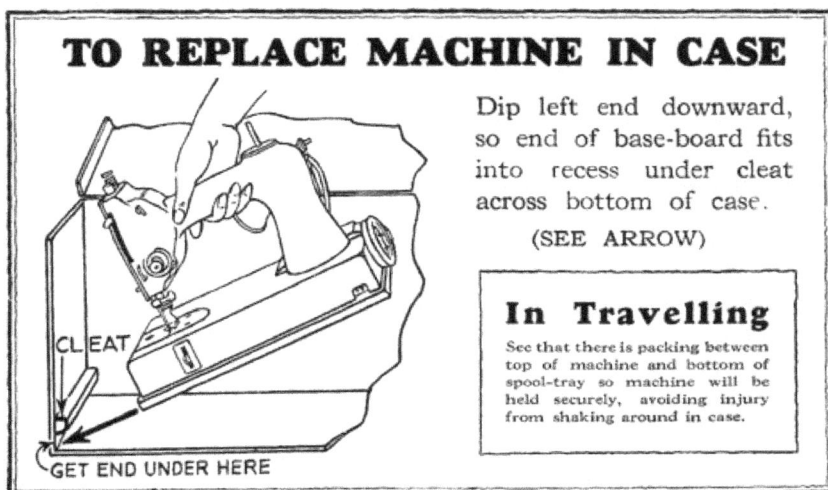

TO REPLACE MACHINE IN CASE

Dip left end downward, so end of base-board fits into recess under cleat across bottom of case.

(SEE ARROW)

In Travelling

See that there is packing between top of machine and bottom of spool-tray so machine will be held securely, avoiding injury from shaking around in case.

CLEAT

GET END UNDER HERE

Form 90   REMOVE THIS PASTER AFTER READING

273

Some well meaning people will put their *Sewhandy* inside the case, and then pour loose foam peanuts or fill to keep it in place. That does keep the machine in place, but those little foam pieces break down and get into all the mechanical machine parts. The foam also melts when exposed to oil and grease.

From a sewing machine technician point-of-view, this is a disaster (and very expensive for you). If you are going to use foam peanuts, bag them in zip-locks or similar before you put them in the case. This will save many future problems.

Some use specially cutout foam pieces to keep their *Sewhandy* in place. However, hard foam vibrating against decals and paint may cause damage.

So how should you protect your *Sewhandy*? Here are some things that need to be done before shipping your machine:
- Remove the spool pin and plate from the top of the *Sewhandy*. If you do not, it will be bent or broken off when the machine gets to the destination. Separately bag it and insert with machine.
- Put soft cotton cloth between the lamp assembly and the *Sewhandy* arm. This prevents the lamp from rubbing against it and damaging the paint and decals.
- Loosely wrap the *Sewhandy* in a plastic bag. This will minimize wear on painted surface from everything. Make sure that

the *Sewhandy* is at room temperature <u>before</u> wrapping it, otherwise it will form condensation and begin to rust.
- Wrap the accessories in bubble wrap and gently place on the machine bed.
- Make sure that the *Sewhandy* front edge is under the restraining board at the bottom of the case.

TO REPLACE MACHINE IN CASE

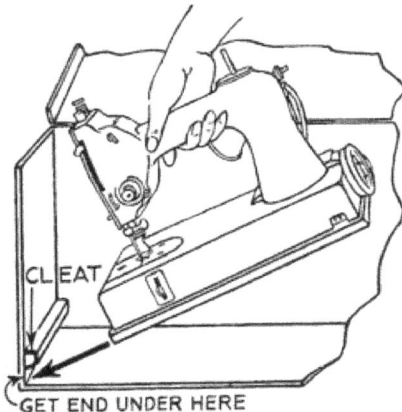

Dip left end downward, so end of base-board fits into recess under cleat across bottom of case.

(SEE ARROW)

CLEAT

GET END UNDER HERE

In Travelling

See that there is packing between top of machine and bottom of spool-tray so machine will be held securely, avoiding injury from shaking around in case.

Form 90   REMOVE THIS PASTER AFTER READING

- Pack the *Sewhandy* snugly into its case. Damage is usually caused by movement inside the case. Any movement at all will cause damage. Some use foam for this. I recommend using soft fabric or cloth.
- Do not put anything heavy into the wooden accessory tray. It will break up the tray when shipped.

- Protect the instruction manual and other paperwork by putting them in a zip lock bag.
- You want the *Sewhandy* to stay in place without moving, but do not over stuff the inside of carrying case. The case top should not require forcing, but easily close. Excessive pressure on the hinges and latches will break them. If the hinges and latches don't give way, then the *Sewhandy* may break thru the bottom.
- When you are finished and with the carrying case closed and latched, shake it and listen for any noises. If you hear something moving around or hitting, open it up and try packing the *Sewhandy* again.
- Wrap the outside of closed case with bubble wrap, and then insert everything in a strong card board shipping box.
- Use more bubble wrap or foam to around the carrying case to securely keep it from moving around inside the shipping box.
- Use enough shipping tape around sides and ends to securely seal the card board shipping box.
- Insure your *Sewhandy*... and ship.

SUMMARY

This brings to a close this book "before the Featherweight – Sewhandy Volume 2 Maintenance and Repair".

I hope that you found reading it both enjoyable and educational.

For more detailed information about the history and the development of the *Sewhandy*, be sure to read my book "before the Featherweight – Sewhandy Volume 1 History". You will find a short preview of Volume 1 beginning on page 283 of this book.

Reference and Bibliography information available on request.

If you have any questions about this book or the Sewhandy sewing machine, visit my website:

www.SewhandySewingMachine.com

You can also email me at **Dar-Bet@att.net** .

For information about other books I have written, visit my website:

www.DarrelKaiserBooks.com

APPENDIX
PERSONAL MACHINE DIARY

DATE	MODEL	SN	PURCHASE INFORMATION

APPENDIX
COMPARISON

GE Sewhandy	Specification	SINGER 221 Featherweight
9-1/4"	Machine Height	9-1/4"
7-1/16"	Machine Width	7-1/4"
11-7/8"	Machine Length	10-1/2"
15.75 lbs	Machine Weight	11.1lbs
5"	Mach throat width	5"
3-5/8"	Mach throat height	4"
2-3/8"	Work Space	6-1/4"
11"	Case Height	11-1/2"
8"	Case Width	8"
13"	Case Length	13"
wood/vinyl	Case construction	wood/vinyl
20.25 lbs	Case+Mach weight	16.1 lbs
AC-DC	Motor Voltage Type	AC-DC
110-120	Motor Voltage	110-120
25-75	Motor AC Cycles	25-75
50	Motor Watts	66
0.4	Motor Amp	0.55
8000	Motor RPM (Load)	3500
11000	Motor RPM (No Load)	7600
Singer	Motor Mfg	Singer
daily(A)	Oil schedule	daily(B)
18(C)	Oil Holes or points	38(D)
No Dial	Top Tension Adj.	Dial
6-20 inch	Stitch length	6-30 inch
1100	Stitches per Minute	850
Fwd	Feed Directions	Fwd-Rev

(A) oil moving parts frequently
(B) daily if continuously used; occasional if moderately used
(C) per page 5 Inst Manual - (c)1934
(D) per pages 24-26 221-1 Instructions Manual - (c)1948

PREVIEW

before the
Featherweight

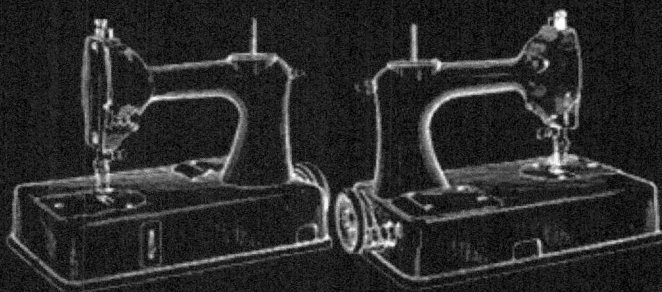

Sewhandy
Volume 1
History

Darrel P. Kaiser

283

Chapter Titles

- **IN THE BEGINNING**

- **THE INVENTOR**

- **HIS "SEWING MACHINE" PATENT**

- **MARKETING**

- **FREDERICK OSANN COMPANY**

- **STANDARD SEWING MACHINE COMPANY**

- **THE *Sewhandy* SEWING MACHINE**

- **STANDARD SEWING MACHINE COMPANY FAILURE**

- **GENERAL ELECTRIC *MODEL A* SEWING MACHINE**

- **SINGER SEWING MACHINE COMPANY**

PREFACE

There has been gossip and speculation that the Standard *"Sewhandy"* machine was possibly the forerunner of the Singer featherweight. This book will settle those rumors with an explanation of all the information presently available.

IN THE BEGINNING

Sewing machines had come a long ways by the 1900's, and once they became electric powered, their appeal to the masses exploded. World War I drew women out of their homes to support the war effort, and exposed them to the new technology. The advertisement below uses this theme to promote portable sewing machines.

"Why that's the same kind of machine that I used at the Red Cross!"

Thousands of women who helped in war-relief work have learned a practical lesson in sewing efficiency. They have learned that by sewing the new way, with the Portable Electric Sewing Machine, they get a great deal more sewing done in less time and with less effort.

Western Electric
Portable Sewing Machine

Portable sewing machine models were available in the early 1920's from a number of different manufacturers, such as SINGER, WHITE, and STANDARD.

The SINGER Sewing Machine Company filed for a US patent on a portable sewing machine before 1920, and introduced the SINGER "portable electric" 99K for sale to the public in 1921.

SINGER Hand Portable

The **SINGER** ad below is a typical of the time up to late 1933.

SEW WHEREVER YOU WISH

You will never know how conven- ient a modern sewing machine can be until you use a Singer Portable Electric. For here is a machine so compact that you can pick it up, carry it, sew with it wherever you wish! And when sewing time is done, your Singer is placed in a closet — out of sight and out of the way.

Only in a genuine Singer do you obtain enduring Singer quality and perfect work- manship. Hidden power under perfect control does all the work. No need even for an extra light—the Singerlight attached to the machine casts its soft rays upon your work, shielding your eyes from glare.

Singer Sewing Machine Co.

INCORPORATED

206 W. Clark St.   Phone 3044

May we give you an interesting demonstration?

288

By 1926, STANDARD Sewing Machine Company of Cleveland had their portable model R72 out for sale. Picture below is a later STANDARD portable.

Most of the portable electric sewing machines were just adaptations of treadle powered table sewing machine designs.

For the sewing machine manufacturers this was a logical next step. Add an electric motor and you now had an electric portable model to sell to the public. However, current electric motors were heavy making the machines weigh even more than the table model.

The typical electric portable of the 1920's was heavy with a carrying weight of over 30 pounds. They may have been called "portable," but you would not want to "port" them very far.

A new lighter and less expensive portable electric sewing machine design was needed. But for the sewing machine manufacturers the important concerns were:

- ## Who could design one?

- ## Would the public buy it?

- ## Would it make them money?

_____

Find out the answers to these questions and many more in the over 200 pages in Volume 1. Visit my websites:

www.SewhandySewingMachine.com

www.DarrelKaiserBooks.com

Books by Darrel P. Kaiser
www.DarrelKaiserBooks.com

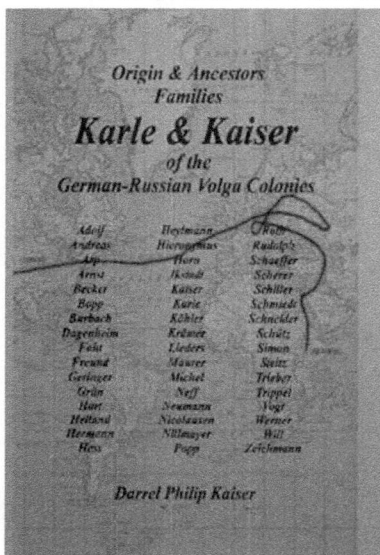

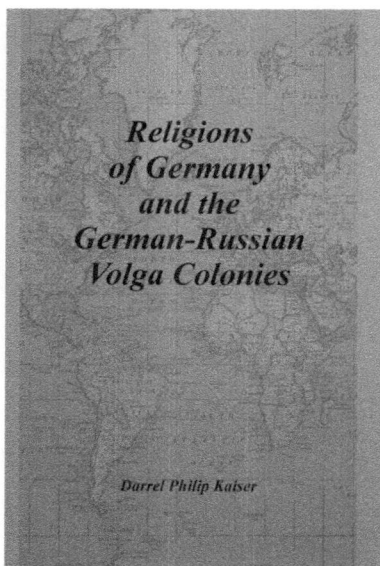

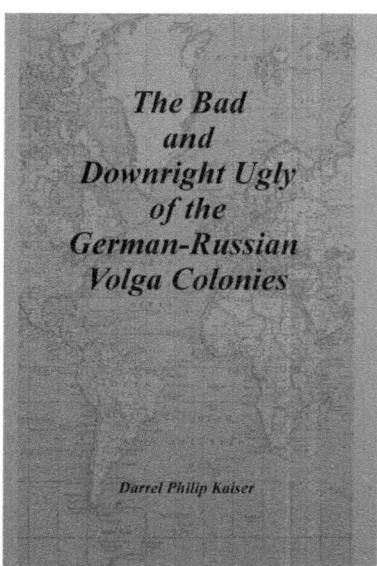

Origin & Ancestors
Families
Karle & Kaiser
of the
German-Russian Volga Colonies

Adolf	Heymann	Roth
Andreas	Hieronimus	Rudolph
App	Horn	Schaeffer
Arnt	Ikandt	Scherer
Becker	Kaiser	Schiller
Bopp	Karle	Schmiede
Barbach	Köhler	Schneider
Dagenheim	Krämer	Schütz
Feist	Lieders	Simon
Freund	Maurer	Seitz
Geringer	Michel	Trieber
Grün	Neff	Trippel
Hart	Neumann	Vogt
Heiland	Nicolausen	Werner
Hermann	Niemayer	Will
Hess	Popp	Zeichmann

Darrel Philip Kaiser

Moscow's
Final Solution:
The Genocide
of the
German-Russian
Volga Colonies

Darrel Philip Kaiser

Religions
of Germany
and the
German-Russian
Volga Colonies

Darrel Philip Kaiser

The Bad
and
Downright Ugly
of the
German-Russian
Volga Colonies

Darrel Philip Kaiser

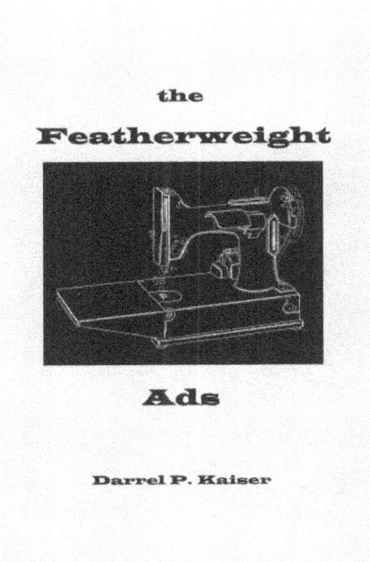

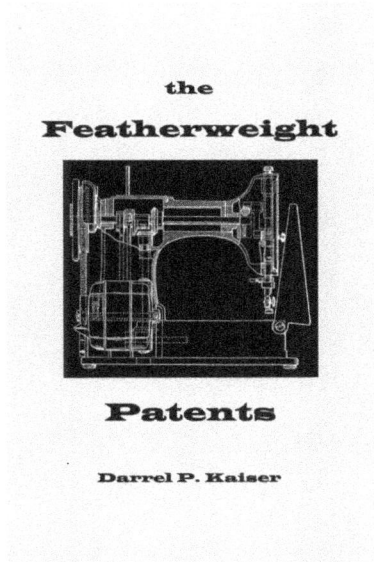

Books by Darrel P. Kaiser
www.DarrelKaiserBooks.com

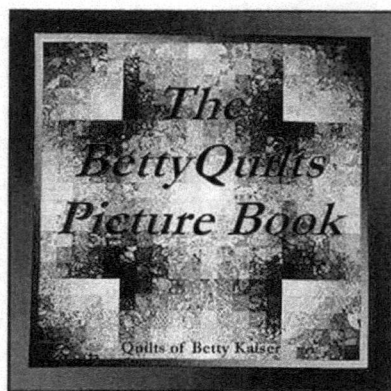

before the
Featherweight

Sewhandy
Volume 1
History

Darrel P. Kaiser

before the
Featherweight

Sewhandy
Volume 2
Maintenance
& Repair

Darrel P. Kaiser

Logical
Sewing Machine
Troubleshooting

ALL BRANDS

ANTIQUE - COMPUTER

for Everyone

Darrel Philip Kaiser

The
BettyQuilts
Picture Book

Quilts of Betty Kaiser

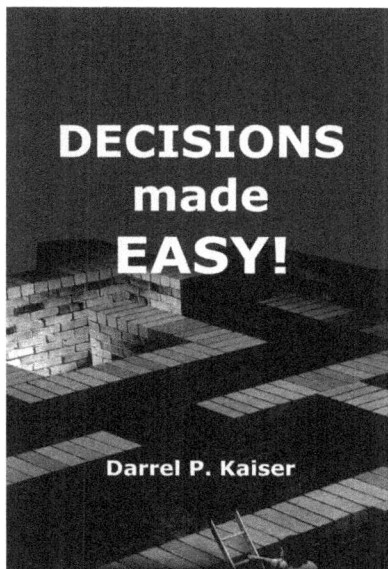

www.ingramcontent.com/pod-product-compliance
Lightning Source LLC
Chambersburg PA
CBHW031558110426
42742CB00036B/239